And the Raven, never flitting, still is sitting, still is sitting

On the pallid bust of Pallas just above my chamber door;

And his eyes have all the seeming of a demon's that is
dreaming,

And the lamp-light o'er him streaming throws his shadow
on the floor;

And my soul from out that shadow that lies floating on the
floor

Shall be lifted

Nevermore!

~ The Raven ~

Edgar Allan Poe ~ 1845~

Unbroken Echoes

A Memoir of Trauma, Healing, and the Echoes Within

by Kelea Ravyn

Author's Note

This memoir is written from memory as I experienced it then and as I understand it now.

Where any uncertainty exists, I have tried to reflect that honestly.

Trauma doesn't organize itself in neat timelines. Some moments stayed with me sharp and clear, and others returned in fragments. Some only made sense to me years later, when I finally had an understanding of what I had lived through.

I have written these chapters honestly from the perspective I held at each stage in my life, while allowing my present voice to reflect what I understand today.

Throughout this book I describe the inner voices I came to call my Echoes. For most of my life I believed they were my imagination, my instinct, or something else I couldn't explain.

Later I was diagnosed with Dissociative Identity Disorder (Multiple Personality Disorder) and started to understand that the echoes were part of how my mind protected me when I didn't have the comprehension of what I was going through.

This book is written to help show Dissociative Identity Disorder in a different light than it is often shown in movies or television. My experience is not dramatic or sensational. It is quiet, complex, and rooted in survival.

I am sharing this story because understanding brought me peace, and because I am hoping maybe it helps others recognize that the mind sometimes creates extraordinary ways to stay alive.

This story isn't only about trauma. It's about survival, understanding, and learning to live beside the parts of myself that carried me when I couldn't carry everything alone.

<u>*Content Note*</u>

This memoir includes references to childhood trauma, including emotional abuse, sexual abuse, family violence, loss, and experiences connected to exploitation and human trafficking.

These events are described without graphic detail, but they may still be difficult for some readers.

This book is written with care and respect for those who have lived through similar experiences.

Readers are encouraged to move through the story at the pace that feels right for them.

~Dedication~

For my beautiful children who are my brightest reflections and who remind me every day that love can grow even from the worst soil. Your laughter rebuilt what the world once tried to take away from me. I am so proud of all of you. I love how you all believe, dream and then achieve. Loves you <3

For my husband, whose patience became a safe place to land. A foundation where I could finally settle. You stood beside me when I was learning how to exist as all of us, and you never asked me to be any less. It takes a special man to go through life with me. I love you

For my mom, who taught me what unconditional love looks like even in some of the darkest moments.

For my uncle, the man who showed me that gentleness and strength can live in the same heart. That compassion is something given not earned. Thank you for being confident in me and for always being my biggest cheerleader.

My brothers that I lost, who loved me through every chapter, who carried pieces of my heart even when life took us in different directions. Your memory lives quietly in every page of my story. I keep you with me always.

To my sister, who chose to love me even when it wasn't easy. Our bond grows stronger every day.

To my cousin, whose energy flows through me and vice versa. You are the steady rock whenever it's needed. You understand me better than anyone. Nevermore.

For my therapist, who never asked me to relive my pain to prove it was real and who met every echo with compassion instead of fear or judgement. Thank you for allowing me to heal with all my echoes.

To my family, extended family, ninja family and for anyone who has been there for me through any of this, thank you! You may never know how much you impacted my life but your kindness became a hand I could hold on to when the world felt too heavy.

This book is for all of you, for every single person who stayed, for every person that made the darkness gentler, and for every whisper of hope that kept me alive long enough to find me again, all of me.

Before the Echoes

There's a moment just before movement begins, the breath you take before you reach the heartbeat and before you finally let go.

I've learned to love that pause. It's the same stillness that carries me through everything now, whether I'm writing, training, coaching, or standing at the edge of something that once would've made me turn back.

There was a time when that pause felt terrifying, when stillness wasn't calm at all but a reminder of all the noise I'd survived. I didn't understand then why my body braced at quiet moments, or why a held breath could feel like both safety and danger at the same time. Silence used to carry questions I couldn't answer and memories I couldn't outrun. Now it's become a place where I can listen without fear of what I might hear.

For most of my life I didn't have words for what was happening inside me. When things became too heavy, something in me answered. Sometimes it sounded like a warning. Sometimes it sounded like anger. Sometimes it sounded like comfort. I call them echoes because that's what they felt like, pieces of myself returning when I needed them most, carrying protection before I understood why I needed it.

I believed strength meant pushing forward without stopping and without looking back. I thought survival meant to keep moving and to not look back. I didn't know then there was a pause that itself was part of my learning how to live.

My story begins there.

It begins in the breath before the leap, in the stillness before the sound returns, in the moment when survival slowly becomes something else. It begins when I finally stopped running from my own mind and started to listen.

Interlude Chapter 1

The Ravenmarked Oak stands in stillness, its great branches bending inward as if they're listening to something deeper than wind.

The flowers at its roots sway in waves that have nothing to do with the breeze. Their petals catch the last threads of daylight and hold them like small lanterns.

The creek beyond them moves with a sound like breathing, steady and low, carrying the kind of quiet that doesn't feel empty. Only watchful.

The air smells of damp earth and moss, of bark warmed by sun and cooled by shadow. The ground beneath the oak is soft with fallen leaves, their edges curled and brown, whispering against each other when the wind finally does arrive.

Echo Guard stands beside the tree trunk, one hand resting flat against the raven carved deep into the bark. His fingers trace the grooves slowly and deliberately, as if reading something written there. His shoulders are square. His spine is straight. He doesn't shift his weight. He simply stands present and grounded, assessing the clearing with eyes that miss nothing. His breath is even and his jaw is set. He isn't cold. He's vigilant. A guardian in the truest sense.

Harmony sits on the bench beneath the branches, her hands folded in her lap, her head tilted slightly as if listening to something just beyond hearing. Her posture is soft but not collapsed. She holds herself gently, the way you might hold something fragile that you're trying not to break.

Vex rocks slowly in the tire swing, one foot dragging through the dirt in lazy circles, leaving shallow grooves in the earth. Her movements are restless but contained, like energy looking for a place to land.

And then there is Ember.

She leans against the tree, but not the way Echo Guard stands. Ember's weight shifts. Her shoulders tense and release, then tense and release again. The outline of her form flickers with a warmth that never fully becomes flame but threatens to at any moment. Heat radiates from her in waves that distort the air around her edges. Her hands curl into fists, then open, then curl again. Her breathing is shallow and quick.

She's raw. Uncontrolled. A fire that hasn't yet learned its own shape.

"She's changing," Harmony says softly, her voice barely louder than the creek.

Vex tilts her head, the swing creaking beneath her. "She thinks it's just sickness"

Ember's jaw tightens. When she speaks, her voice comes out rough, like something scraped against stone.

"It is sickness. It's just not only that."

Her hands flex again, and for a moment the air around her shimmers with heat.

Echo Guard's gaze doesn't leave the path leading into the clearing. His hand remains steady against the carved raven.

"She's about to lose something," he says, his voice low and certain. Not a prediction, an assessment.

Harmony lowers her gaze to the violet flowers at her feet, their petals trembling though the air has gone still.

"And gain something too," she whispers.

Above them, the raven in the branches shifts once, a rustle of dark wings against darker leaves, a sound like paper folding. Then it settles again, watching with eyes that catch the fading light.

The clearing holds its breath.

Echo Guard's fingers press more firmly against the bark, feeling the grain of it, the solidity. His voice when it comes is quiet but carries through the space like a stone dropped into still water.

"Listen," he says. "This is where the silence begins."

I

The First Breath of Freedom

The page waits quietly in front of me as if it already knows what I'm afraid to remember. The pen feels heavier than it should, and the air around me tightens in my chest as though memory itself has weight. I tell myself I'm only writing and that words are only words, but memory has a way of breathing once you let it out.

A small voice inside me says, "Just write it."

Another voice answers, "Not yet."

And then a softer one asks, "What if you remember it wrong?"

I promise myself I'll only write what feels safe, even though safety has never been something I fully understood. Every memory I carry holds its own ghosts, and every silence hides a sound I once heard louder than actual noise. That is where I should begin. With the moment the silence began.

The world didn't go quiet all at once. It faded slowly, like a sound interrupted mid sentence, a conversation the universe forgot to finish.

I was sick and caught in a fever that refused to break. The hospital room smelled of bleach and wet towels, and the air was thick with my mother's worry. My skin felt cold and hot at the same time. Pain pulsed through my ear with every heartbeat until the ache started to become its own rhythm.

Then came the blood. It ran hot and sticky down my neck while voices drifted all around me. My mother's voice sounded sharp with panic, and another voice tried to stay calm as it spoke words like infection and swelling and antibiotics. I heard someone say my name, but it sounded far away, as if it was being spoken underwater. I tried to answer, but my tongue felt too heavy and my body wouldn't move. The world spun, and I remember getting sick.

When the fever peaked, I started seeing things I couldn't explain. The ceiling shimmered like water. Shadows moved slowly along the walls in ways that didn't match the room. I saw a man's outline appear near the window and disappear as soon as I blinked. Maybe it was only the fever, or maybe it was something else.

I remember at one point feeling like I was floating above myself. The child in the bed looked so small and fragile. Her body was drenched in sweat, and her mouth was open in a silent cry. I wanted to reach down and pull her somewhere safer, but I couldn't move. The pain became light. The light became silence.

Fragments from that time still return in strange pieces, as if someone shook my memory like a snow globe and let them settle in different places each time I look at them. I remember the faded blue curtain that covered the window and the way it moved whenever the door opened. I remember the hallway outside the room feeling colder than the air inside. I remember wanting to run into that hallway even though I didn't understand why.

Even small things felt enormous. I remember how much I didn't like the buzzing lights overhead and the stillness between them.

Time stretched until I couldn't tell whether minutes or hours were passing by. Sometimes the world dimmed so suddenly that it felt like someone had flicked a switch inside my body. During those moments I felt something steady beside me. It wasn't someone I could see or name. It was just a presence that stayed when everything else seemed to drift away.

I didn't know then that I would feel that same steadiness again later in my life. It felt like breathing with someone who wasn't touching me. I held onto that feeling longer than I held onto consciousness.

There is another memory from that time that never fully settles into place. I remember that there was a fight. I remember the sting on my cheek and the terror I felt from my stepfather's rage. The sound of the ornaments falling when the Christmas tree was knocked over is a sound I still can't get rid of.

I don't know whether that moment was connected to what happened to my hearing or if they only live beside each other in my memory because they both frightened me so much. We lived in that house for two years, and I have very little memory from that time.

There is time from that house that surfaces in fragments, the way trauma sometimes does, pieces that don't quite fit together but refuse to disappear.

My mother had gone bowling. The house felt quieter without her, the air thicker. My stepfather stayed home, and I kept my distance the way I had learned to do. He made comments sometimes, touches that felt wrong in ways I couldn't name yet. So I stayed small and tried to be invisible.

Jeffrey was just a baby then, still in casts from his hip surgery. The white plaster covered both his legs, heavy and awkward, but he didn't seem to mind. He loved the waterbed in my mother's room, the way it moved beneath him like gentle waves. I would press my hands into the mattress and watch him giggle, his whole face lighting up with joy. That sound was one of the few pure things in that house.

I made the waves bigger, and his laughter grew louder. For a moment, everything felt safe. For a moment, I forgot to be afraid.

Then he rolled.

It happened so fast. One second he was laughing, the next he was tumbling toward the edge. I lunged for him but wasn't quick enough. He hit the floor with a thud that seemed to shake the whole room, and immediately his cry pierced the air, sharp, terrified, hurting.

I scooped him up as fast as I could, cradling his casted legs carefully, pulling him against my chest.

"It's okay," I whispered, rocking him gently. "You're okay. I've got you."

My heart was pounding, not just from the fall, but from what I knew was coming.

The footsteps came fast and heavy down the hallway.

I knew that sound. I knew what it meant. My stomach dropped, and something inside me went very still, very cold. I held Jeffrey tighter and started backing away from the door, my body already preparing to run. He grabbed Jeffrey and started hugging him tightly.

Then his voice exploded into the room, my name, bellowed with rage. I froze. I turned and saw his face.

I tried to move, tried to get away, but my legs wouldn't obey fast enough. His foot came up and connected with my stomach before I could even raise my hands. The impact drove all the air from my lungs in a single violent rush. I flew backward, my body weightless before I slammed into the door frame.

Stars burst across my vision. White and sharp and blinding.

I couldn't breathe. My chest tried to pull in air, but nothing came. I gasped, mouth open, lungs screaming, but the breath wouldn't return. Panic flooded through me, not just from the pain, but from the suffocation, the terror of my body refusing to work. I clutched at my stomach, bent forward, trying to force the air back in.

Jeffrey was still crying somewhere nearby. I wanted to reach for him, to make sure he was okay, but I couldn't move. I couldn't think. I couldn't breathe.

When the air finally came back, it came in jagged, desperate gulps.

My ribs ached. My back throbbed where it had hit the frame. But worse than the pain was the understanding settling into my bones. I hadn't seen it coming. There had been no warning, no buildup. Just noise, and then violence.

I learned something in that moment, something I shouldn't have had to learn. I learned that safety was an illusion, tenderness could be punished and I needed to be ready for anything, because the world could turn on me in an instant.

Something inside me shifted then, though I didn't know what it was. I could never quite put a finger on it. A quiet presence pressed closer, steadying me when my own legs wouldn't hold. It felt like a hand on my shoulder, invisible but firm. Like someone whispering, *I'm here. I'll help you carry this.*

I didn't know then that my mind was already learning how to split the weight of what I couldn't carry alone. I didn't know that this moment, and all the others like it, were teaching me how to exist in more than one place at once. How to be the girl gasping for air on the floor and also the one standing just outside herself, watching, waiting, surviving.

All I knew was that I couldn't tell anyone. Not about the kick. Not about the fear. Not about any of it.

Silence didn't empty me. It left me with echoes.

Dear younger self,

I know you thought the silence meant something had been taken from you. And you're right in some ways, it did. But it also made room for something else, something you won't understand for many years.

You were not becoming weird or crazy. You were becoming skilled at survival.

Every whisper that rose inside you, every presence you felt in the quiet, every strange kind of comfort that arrived when the world turned dark, all of it was your mind refusing to let you disappear.

You are not broken in this chapter of your life. I know how hard this is to believe but you're adapting in ways no child should ever have to.

One day you'll stop being afraid of the echoes. One day you'll hear them for what they always were, love, protection, hope, and the first signs that you were never alone inside yourself.

Love, Me xoxo

The creek moves beneath the Ravenmarked Oak, but tonight its sound is different, sharper and faster, like something running away. The water catches on stones and splinters into white foam before rushing onward, refusing to slow and refusing to settle.

The air is cool but not cold, carrying the scent of damp earth and something else, something like the moment before a storm breaks, when the sky holds its breath and the world goes still with waiting.

The violet flowers at the oak's roots bend low, their petals trembling though there is no wind. They fold inward as if trying to protect something fragile at their centers. The ground beneath them is soft, almost too soft, like it is preparing to absorb what is coming.

Echo Guard stands beside the carved raven, one hand pressed flat against the bark. His fingers trace the grooves slowly and deliberately, reading the wood like braille. His shoulders are square. His spine is straight. There is tension in his jaw, a tightness that was not there before. He is assessing. Calculating.

His eyes scan the clearing, the path, and the shadows between the trees. He is preparing for impact, bracing himself and the others for the wound that is about to open.

Harmony kneels among the flowers, her hands hovering just above the petals but not quite touching. Her head is bowed and her breathing shallow. She rocks slightly forward and back, forward and back, as if trying to soothe something that has not arrived yet but she can already feel. Her shoulders curve inward, protective, cradling an invisible grief. She knows what is coming. She can feel it in the way the air has changed, in the way the flowers bend, and in the way the earth beneath her knees seems to soften in preparation.

Vex paces near the tire swing, her movements sharp and restless. She does not sit. She cannot. Her feet trace the same path over and over, three steps forward, pivot, three steps back. Her hands flex and release, flex and release. She kicks at loose stones, sending them skittering across the clearing. The swing creaks behind her, swaying slightly from where she brushed against it. She is all motion, all kinetic energy looking for somewhere to land, somewhere to run.

And then there is Ember.

She stands near the edge of the clearing where the path disappears into darkness, and the air around her shimmers with heat. Not controlled. Not modulated. Raw. The outline of her form flickers and distorts, like looking at something through rising steam. Her hands are clenched into fists so tightly her knuckles would be white if she were solid. Her breathing comes fast and shallow, each exhale visible as a ripple of heat in the cooling air.

When she speaks, her voice cracks like kindling catching fire.

"He's leaving," she says. "He's leaving and she doesn't even know yet that he's never coming back."

Harmony's rocking intensifies slightly.

"She'll wait for him," she whispers to the flowers. "She'll wait so long."

"And he won't come."

Ember's voice rises, heat radiating from her in waves that make the violet flowers nearest to her curl at the edges.

"He won't even try. He'll just go."

Her hands open and close again and again, like she is trying to hold onto something already slipping away.

Vex stops pacing long enough to kick the base of the tire swing hard. It lurches sideways, the rope groaning.

"So we run," she says, her voice tight. "We keep moving. We do not let it catch us."

"It already caught her."

Echo Guard's voice is low and steady, but there is an edge to it, something protective and fierce. His hand presses harder against the carved raven.

"She's about to learn what leaving feels like."

Ember turns sharply, and the heat around her flares.

"It feels like burning," she says. "It feels like your chest is on fire and you can't breathe and nobody cares that you're choking on it."

The air between them grows warmer. The creek's rushing sound seems louder now and more insistent.

Harmony lifts her head, tears streaming down her face though she makes no sound.

"This is where absence becomes a wound," she says softly, her voice breaking on the last word.

Echo Guard's jaw tightens. He doesn't move from his position beside the tree, but his presence seems to expand.

"Then we stay," he says, his voice carrying the weight of a vow. "We hold her through it."

Ember's fists shake. The heat around her pulses, uncontrolled and wild.

"I want to make him feel it," she says. "I want him to burn the way she is going to burn."

"He won't," Vex mutters, resuming her pacing. "They never do."

Above them, the raven shifts in the branches, a rustle of dark wings, a low sound that might be warning or witness. He watches intently as the Echoes discuss what they need to do next. The clearing holds its breath.

The temperature drops slightly, and the creek's sound changes again, less rushing now and more like weeping. The earth beneath them seems to settle, preparing itself to hold the weight of a child's first real abandonment.

Echo Guard's fingers trace the raven one more time, then he straightens, his shoulders pulling back.

"Listen," he says quietly, but his voice carries through the clearing like a stone dropped into still water. "This is where absence becomes a wound."

Ember's heat flares one more time, bright and fierce and completely uncontained.

"Then we stay," Harmony whispers to the flowers, to the earth, and to the air itself.

And no one argues.

II

The First Sound of Silence

There is always a heartbeat before the echo. There is a breath held between the moment sound begins and the silence that remembers what it was before.

I was born in the summer heat of Ontario in 1975. My mom said I was planned and loved but I think we were both misled by promises neither of us understood. When my parents separated my father traded bedtime stories for a bottle and a bar stool. He left behind empty drawers and the absence of any explanation.

I used to believe people left the way they left an argument only temporarily. I asked my mom often when he was coming back. My mother said he just needed some time. I gave it time. Weeks became months and the space where his voice used to live filled with a strange ringing quiet.

I asked again.

"Why did he go?"

No one answered.

"Did I do something wrong?"

Still nothing.

At night I whispered my questions to the ceiling, the window and the thin slice of moon hovering above the backyard. Maybe he could hear me through the stars. Maybe he was asking his own questions about me. Maybe we were looking at the same sky wondering the same things.

Sometimes when I asked I felt something shift inside me like air moving in a sealed jar. A flicker of warmth appeared. A hush that was not entirely my own.

One night a small voice brushed my ear.

"You didn't do anything."

I froze.

"Who said that?"

No one answered but the fear loosened.

The next night the whisper came again softer.

"Sleep now."

I started talking to the air as if someone lived in it. Maybe it was God or a guardian angel. Maybe it was the part of me that refused to vanish. I knew something or someone was always with me even if I could not fully understand it.

My father never wrote, never called and never made any attempt to visit me that I knew of. Years later I learned he signed the papers that allowed my stepfather to adopt me.

I didn't know whether he understood what kind of man he was signing me over to. I didn't know whether he even cared enough to find out. He gave me away with less reassurance than a person lending their lawnmower to their neighbour. To him I was not a daughter, I was an inconvenience he passed along. I would love to tell you there was a heartfelt goodbye but there wasn't.

He left and the world didn't pause for me.

I stayed close with his family, his parents and especially his brother, my uncle. They were the fragments of him that remained in my life.

One weekend when I was about fourteen I was at my grandparents' house. The air smelled of cake and icing. My uncle put on his record and we were listening to In the Air Tonight by Phil Collins.

I noticed a photo of two boys who strongly resembled our family.

"Who are they?" I asked

My uncle stiffened.

"Hold on," he said and left the room.

The record kept spinning and the song grew faint in the background. My grandmother entered drying her hands on a towel.

"Those are your brothers," she said quietly.

I stared at the photo. Two whole lives no one had told me about. Five years of birthdays, holidays and moments swallowed by silence.

The song reached the drum solo loud and certain and I remember thinking that was what truth sounded like when it finally arrived.

That night I lay awake listening to the record spin in my mind. A whisper rose inside me.

"You are not the one who disappeared."

Another answered from deeper still.

"But we did in a way."

I didn't know what that meant but the silence inside me was no longer empty. It hummed with presence.

Time bends in memory and suddenly the other man who became my father legally fills the doorway, my stepfather. His voice is too big for the room and his laughter scrapes the ceiling. Even the light seems to shrink when he enters. I learn to read him the way others read books, through tone silence and the rhythm of his footsteps. When the air changes my stomach tightens and I move before he speaks.

At first he calls me sweetheart or lovebug in a voice that makes my mother smile. Later those same words turned sharp.

The first time his anger erupts it feels like watching weather form. My mother's voice goes quiet and her eyes search for an escape. I stand frozen and the world narrows to the sound of his breathing. Inside me something moves. A ripple of stillness spreads outward calm and cold. A hand not quite physical presses against my heart.

"Stay still," a voice murmurs.

I obey. The air steadies and the noise blurs.

I can remember having a headache and bruises on my wrists, and I know why but when I think of it I feel like I'm watching it happen to someone else.

Afterwards I hide in my room.

"Who are you?"

The answer comes like breath against glass.

"I am the quiet between the cracks."

I think of this presence as a guardian spirit part dream part echo. They don't tell me their name. Only that they exist when I need them most.

At school life continues as if nothing has happened. I sit near the window and chalk squeaks across the board like tiny screams. The teacher calls on me and I hesitate lost in thought. Laughter ripples across the room. They always find a reason to laugh at me.

A new voice surfaces inside me, light, quick and full of practiced charm.

"Smile. If they laugh with you they cannot laugh at you."

So I smile. I mimic their laughter until it almost feels real.

At recess when others run and shout I wander to the fence and trace its cold metal diamonds with my fingers. The wind hums through the openings like a tune only I can hear. A small shadow follows beside mine.

"You don't have to talk if you don't want to. Just know that I'm here."

"I'm fine," I answer even though I know that's not true.

At night when everything quiets, the dreams return. In my dreams the voices have faces now soft shimmering outlines that shift like candlelight. One crouches beside the bed tracing patterns in the air.

"Count your breaths," she says.

Another perches by the window with bright mischievous eyes.

"We could run away. Just fly out there."

I never tell anyone about them. To me they are imaginary friends. To them I am someone worth saving.

As the months turn to years their presence becomes part of the landscape. Walking home from school I sense them trailing behind like sunlight shifting through leaves. When I'm scared the air thickens as if someone is holding it still for me. When I laugh the laughter echoes twice.

At home I am expected to keep quiet, stay invisible and agree with everything. I speak softly. I try to smile at the right time. My stepfather's moods come and go like the weather. The smallest thing can change everything.

My mother becomes smaller when he's angry. Her shoulders curl inward and her voice thins. She tries to pretend everything is fine. I watch her movements closely and memorize the rhythm of her survival. Children sometimes learn lessons they were never meant to learn.

I start believing quietness can be a protection and silence becomes armor.

My footsteps soften and my words shrink. When I hear him in the hallway I hold my breath without meaning to. Something inside me braces preparing for impact. Each time a presence rises and steadies me.

Inside the echoes deepen. They don't argue so much as they negotiate. One softens fear. Another stands firm. One whispers reassurance. Another whispers readiness. The calm one brings silence that feels almost sacred. I don't yet understand that this is how they protect me.

Sometimes I look in the mirror and wonder which version of me people see. The frightened girl? The smiling girl? The one who disappears entirely. I don't know. I only know I am never just one self at a time.

One afternoon in fourth grade a boy shoves me as I bend to pick up a pencil. The class laughs and my cheeks burn. I expect silence inside me but warmth rises instead.

"Stand up straight."

Another voice adds

"Don't let them see you sad."

Later that afternoon sitting alone by the coat hooks the cheerful echo appears again.

"They're bored, not brave. You can outlast bored people."

I smile not because I feel better but because she believes in me.

This belief carries me through the early years. It isn't confidence but companionship. An inner presence reminding me I don't have to carry everything alone.

Back at home the storms continue. These are always loud and are aimed at me. On quiet days I almost forget to be afraid. On loud days I forget how to breathe. I'm lucky the echoes never forget. They stay in ways no one else can or will.

One night my stepfather's shouting fills the house. My mother whispers my name from across the room telling me to stay still. I do.

A soft humming begins in my chest. The calm one steps forward.

My heart slows and my breath steadies.

Later alone in my room I press my palms against my cheeks.

"Thank you," I whisper.

The reply is gentle.

"Rest."

Another year passes. I grow but I don't grow any louder. I just become better at pretending and better at hiding how much noise lives inside my silence.

One afternoon walking through the fall leaves from the maple tree I ask inside

"Are you still with me?"

A warmth answers immediately.

"Always."

The leaves crunch beneath my feet like quiet applause.

Winter brings more storms but inside me something else begins to form. It isn't fear and it isn't obedience. It feels more like strength that's gathering quietly.

On the bad nights the echoes feel closer to me.

I lie in bed staring at the faint glow beneath the door and imagine them sitting near the foot of the bed guarding the space between me and the world.

In one dream I ask their names.

Echo Guard places a hand on my shoulder.

"You will name us when you are ready."

Years pass in small increments. Through it all the echoes shift and rearrange as needed. They learn about me as I learn about them. They hold the moments where my voice can't go.

One night the house is very quiet.

I turn to the space beside me and whisper

"Why me."

A new voice answers softly and firmly.

"Because you needed us."

"And you needed me," Echo Guard adds.

I feel a sense of belonging that the outside world has never given me.

Echo Guard appears again faint and luminous at the foot of the bed.

"The world won't understand us," they whisper.

"What won't they understand,?" I ask.

"That wholeness was never about being one thing. It was about being many and loving and accepting every piece."

Outside dawn rises and spills light across the floorboards. Birds test their morning voices. For the first time I didn't flinch at sound. It feels like an answer returning from a long distance.

Every echo begins with a sound, but what begins the echo itself?

I was already answering long before I found the courage to speak about it.

The first sound of silence wasn't an ending at all but the beginning of everything that would one day learn to say, *"We are here."*

Little one,

I wish I could sit beside you right now.

I don't mean in the loud rooms where adults speak in careful voices, and not in the places where you are trying to understand things that were never meant for a child to carry. Just somewhere quiet. Maybe on the floor with your knees pulled up to your chest, the way you sit when the world feels too big.

I wouldn't ask you questions. You've already been asked too many. Instead I would tell you something you need to hear. You are not the problem. I know it feels like you must be, but that is wrong.

When adults are angry, when their voices get sharp, when the air in a room changes quickly it feels like a storm rolling in, children learn to blame themselves first.

What did I do wrong?
What could I have done differently?
How do I make it stop?

You are trying so hard to understand the rules of a game no one ever explained. But the truth is this, you didn't cause the storm. You're just learning how to survive it.

Right now you're becoming something stronger than you realize. You're learning how to listen carefully. How to read the space between words. How to feel the shift in a room before anyone else notices it.

That isn't failure or weakness, that is survival.

One day you will understand that your mind is already building ways to protect you. Quiet and invisible ways. Parts of you that will stand watch when you are too tired to keep your eyes open. You won't know their names yet, but they will be there.

Some will be strong and steady.
Some will be soft and full of feeling.
Some will burn bright when the world tries to dim you.

They will arrive when you need them. Not because you are broken, but because you are determined to live. You will spend years wondering why you feel things so deeply. Why the world sometimes feels too loud or too sharp or too heavy, but that depth inside you will become one of the most powerful parts of who you are and who you become. It will allow you to love fiercely. You will see pain in others when they can't name it themselves. Eventually you will build a life that feels warm and real after so many cold places.

You are going to meet people who love you in ways that feel stable. You're going to build a home filled with laughter. You're going to learn that family is not only the people we are joined with by blood, and that sometimes it is the people we build our lives beside. And one day you will begin to understand the quiet voices that helped you survive.

You will realize they were never enemies. They were guardians.

You are not alone, ever!

I know sometimes you're scared. I know there's nights when the world feels too confusing and you wish someone would just explain it all. I can't change what you are about to walk through, but I can promise you this:

You will survive it.

You will grow through it.

You will learn to name the things that once felt impossible to understand.

You will build a life that feels brighter than anything you can imagine right now.

And one day you will look back at the little girl sitting on that floor and realize something extraordinary.

She never gave up. You can do this.

I am here.

With love,
Your future self xxoo

The clearing beneath the Ravenmarked Oak is smaller tonight.

Not because the trees have moved closer, but because the air itself has thickened, heavy with something unspoken, something waiting. The earth beneath them feels softer than before, almost too soft, as if preparing to absorb weight it knows is coming.

The creek beyond the clearing runs quieter now, its sound muted and distant, like it's pulling back to give the space room to breathe. The temperature has dropped. Not cold exactly, but cooler than it should be. The kind of cool that settles into your bones and makes you aware of your own skin.

Mist curls along the ground in slow, deliberate waves, slipping between roots and stones with the patience of something that has all the time in the world. It doesn't rush. It doesn't retreat. It simply waits.

The raven watches from its branch above, feathers pulled tight against its body. Its eyes track movement at the edge of the clearing, small, hesitant and curious.

A girl steps out from between the trees.

She is younger here, much younger. Her shoulders are stiff, pulled up toward her ears as if bracing for impact. Her hands hang at her sides, fingers curled slightly inward, uncertain what they're meant to hold or protect. Her breathing is shallow, quick little inhales that don't quite fill her lungs. She takes one step forward, then stops. Her rain boots press into the soft earth, leaving small impressions that slowly fill with mist.

She looks around the clearing with wide eyes. Confusion and recognition move across her face at the same time. This place feels familiar yet not, all at the same time. Like a dream half remembered. Like something she's been searching for without knowing what she was looking for.

The tire swing creaks once, a low lonely sound, and the girl's head snaps toward it.

"Hello?" she whispers.

The word disappears into the trees. No one answers.

But something shifts.

The air behind her changes. It becomes warmer, steadier, and more solid. A presence takes shape just beyond her line of sight. Tall. Still. Watchful. Not threatening, but protective. The girl doesn't turn around, but her shoulders drop slightly. Her breathing slows. She feels it.

Echo Guard stands there now, one hand resting against the carved raven in the oak's trunk. Their outline is faint but growing clearer with each passing moment. Their posture is grounded, feet planted firmly in the earth, spine straight. They don't move toward the girl. They simply stand, present, vigilant, assessing the clearing with eyes that miss nothing. Their jaw is set. Their gaze is steady. They aren't cold. They're ready.

Near the edge of the clearing, another presence flickers into being, restless, bright, pacing the boundary like a spark searching for kindling. Ember's form shimmers with heat that distorts the air around her edges. She doesn't stand still. She can't. Her hands curl into fists, then open, then curl again. Her breathing is quick and shallow. She moves along the tree line, back and forth, radiating warmth that pushes against the cooling air.

By the creek, barely visible in the mist, Harmony kneels among the stones. Her hands hover just above the water's surface but don't quite touch. Her head is bowed, her shoulders curved inward as if cradling something fragile. She rocks slightly forward and back in a gentle motion that seems to soothe the air around her. She knows what's coming. She can feel it in the way the flowers bend, in the way the earth has softened, in the way the clearing itself seems to be holding its breath.

Vex appears near the tire swing, her movements sharp and quick. She doesn't sit. She paces three steps one way, pivots, then three steps back. Her hands flex and release, flex and release. She kicks at loose pebbles, sending them skittering across the clearing. The swing creaks behind her, swaying where she brushed against it. She's all motion, all kinetic energy with nowhere to land.

And somewhere in the shadows, barely more than a glow of pale blue light, Luna watches. Fragile. Tender. Hopeful in a way that feels almost painful. She doesn't step forward yet. She simply holds the space with her presence, her light trembling like a candle flame in a draft.

The girl in the center of the clearing turns slowly, taking in the space around her. She doesn't see them clearly, not yet, but she feels them. The warmth at her back. The heat along the tree line. The gentleness of the water. The restless motion near the swing. The soft glow in the shadows.

She wraps her arms around herself, small fingers gripping her own elbows.

"I don't understand," she whispers to the clearing.

Echo Guard's hand presses more firmly against the carved raven.

"You will," they say quietly. "When you need to."

The girl's breathing hitches. She looks toward the path that leads deeper into the trees, the path that will take her to the new house, the new stepfather, the new kind of fear.

Ember stops pacing. Her heat flares once, bright and fierce.

Harmony's rocking slows but doesn't stop.

Vex's hands still, just for a moment.

Luna's glow brightens slightly, then dims again.

Above them all, the raven shifts its weight from one foot to the other. Its eyes never leave the girl.

The clearing knows what's coming.

The echoes know what's coming.

And they gather, not to speak yet, but to stand witness. To be present. To prepare themselves to hold what she can't hold alone.

The girl takes one more step toward the center of the clearing, then stops. She looks up at the oak, at the raven carved into its trunk, at the branches that bend inward as if they're listening.

"I'm scared," she whispers.

Echo Guard's outline becomes more solid.

"We know."

Ember's heat pulses once.

"We're here."

Harmony's voice drifts across the clearing like mist.

"You're not alone."

Vex stops moving entirely.

"We won't let you disappear."

Luna's glow steadies.

"We promise."

The girl doesn't understand the words yet. She doesn't know their names. She doesn't know what they are or why they're here.

But she feels them.

And for the first time in a long time, the fear in her chest loosens just enough to let her breathe.

The clearing holds its breath.

The echoes stand ready.

And the girl, small, afraid, but not alone, takes one more step forward into the space that will become her sanctuary.

~III~

The First Wound

The new house smells like someone else's past. Dust and paint trying hard to erase what came before. Everyone says new means better, but even as boxes crowd the corners, I can feel it. The quiet has already arrived, slipping through the walls and curling itself into the edges of the room like a secret waiting to be remembered.

My room is bigger this time. I have the basement area to use for myself where I can play games and watch TV. The floorboards creak in a softer rhythm, but they still whisper the same warnings. It should feel safe but it doesn't. The silence here learns my name way too fast.

She is there again, the child, perched on the edge of the bed, knees tucked tight, small fingers gripping the blanket until it wrinkles beneath her palms. Her eyes dart toward every sound in the hallway, every flicker of light under the door.

Echo Guard waits by the window, their outline faint and trembling in the afternoon glow. They have followed us here, not by choice but by need. Their form hovers between breath and shadow, made of fear and the hope that hasn't died yet.

The child looks up at them, her voice a whisper of disbelief.

"I thought moving would fix it."

"It doesn't fix it," Echo Guard tells her softly. *"It only changes the walls."*

Somewhere in the house, a door slams too hard. The sound slices through the air. She flinches, shoulders folding inward, her heartbeat pounding louder than the echo that caused it.

Echo Guard moves closer, their light reaching toward her like a hand that cannot quite touch. They can't stop what is coming, not yet, but they make a small place where she can breathe.

The footsteps in the hallway are not safe. The air thickens. It doesn't need words to tell her what is next.

She curls tighter. "It followed us," she whispers.

"I know," Echo guard says quietly. *"It always does."*

They crouch near the bed, their glow pulsing weakly against the growing dark. They try to hold the air still, to make it stop, but the walls are already learning silence.

The child doesn't cry. She presses her face into the blanket and waits. And in that waiting, the first true echo begins, the one that says run inside yourself until it is over.

Echo Guard lowers their head, not in defeat but in understanding. Their light hardens, becoming the first piece of armor.

Sometimes, after nights like that, when the air still smelled of fear, I would feel something near me, soft, almost shy. The mattress would dip as if a friend had sat down, though no one was there. I told myself they were my invisible friends, the kind other kids imagined for games and secrets. They never asked me to play. They only stayed until the trembling slowed.

They whispered things I didn't understand then, tiny words carrying warmth. Words like breathe, you are still here, morning will come. I thought it was pretend. I didn't know it was the beginning of everything that would save me.

Shadows crawled along the walls, stretching thin fingers across the floor at night time. The child doesn't move, still small, still hidden beneath the blanket. The silence in the house deepens. It's listening now. Every sound has meaning. Every pause is something more.

Down the hall, a voice rises, too loud, too close. Another answers, sharper. Then footsteps.

Echo Guard steps between her and the door. Their glow sharpens into faint lines of silver, light trembling like a drawn blade. They are learning too, they are learning how to become solid when the world demands it.

"Will it hurt again?" the child asks, her voice trembling.

They wanted to tell her no, but memory catches the lie in their throat.

Echo Guard can't speak. Their shape brightens, expanding until the ceiling flickers with their light. For one brief second, the room feels sealed, held safe inside a shimmer of warmth. But it's fragile.

The door opens and brakes the air.

Everything small and sacred puts itself away.

The child disappears inside herself the way a body exhales underwater. Sound fades but the body stays. The mind is racing. Echo Guard follows, wrapping her in quiet, carrying her to a place no one else can reach.

Inside that silence, there are no words, only pulse and memory, a rhythm built for survival. Echo Guard keeps the rhythm steady, holding her afloat until the storm passes.

When it is finally still, the house exhales. The air smells of sweat, fear, and something sour. But she is breathing. She is trembling but she is alive.

Echo Guard kneels beside her. Their light is faint but steady. They don't leave when the danger does. They will never leave her again.

She opens her eyes and whispers, "You stayed."

And though Echo Guard doesn't speak, the answer settles in the air between them.

Always.

Outside, the morning looks ordinary, but the walls know better. Every house after this will remember. Every room will have corners that hum with their silence.

Deep inside, a promise has been made.

If no one else comes, Echo Guard will.

Morning comes too soon, bright and unkind. Sunlight slips through the blinds, cutting the room into stripes of light and shadow. Dust drifts in the air, floating weightless, unaware of what it hovers above.

The child lies still beneath the blanket, pretending to sleep. Pretending feels safer than waking.

Footsteps return, calm as if nothing happened. The smell of coffee seeps under the door, bitter and ordinary.

Echo Guard waits beside the bed. Worried because danger hides better in daylight.

Finally, she sits up. The blanket slides to her lap. Her throat burns, her chest aches from too much stillness. The world outside the door feels too large, too terrifying.

"Do I have to go out there?" she whispers.

Echo Guard doesn't move. He doesn't have to, she already knows the answer.

Downstairs, the voice that hurt her laughs. Even the sound of happiness makes her feel nauseous.

"I don't feel real," she says.

"That's how we stay safe," I whisper from years ahead of her.

She rises, moving through the morning like a ghost. Her motions practiced, mechanical, a puppet that has learned grace. She masters the choreography of survival: smile, nod, answer, disappear. The silence clings to her skin, invisible but tight.

At breakfast, no one notices. The conversation is small talk and weather, the delusion of normal. She answers when spoken to, hands folded, voice even.

Inside, everything hums with unspoken truth. Echo Guard keeps count. One breath at a time. One room at a time. One day closer to night again.

When it is finally quiet, she slips upstairs. Her hands shake, but she closes the door softly, always softly. She sits on the bed. Echo Guard's light steadies.

She doesn't ask if they will come tonight. They already know.

And in that shared knowing, something fragile forms. Not healing or wholeness, but persistence.

She's still here.

Days pass and the bruises fade, slowly, in uneven colors that seem to never really disappear. The house pretends to settle. Outside, sprinklers tick across the grass, neighbors laugh, mail drops through the slot. Inside, the walls still breathe her name.

She moves through hallways with practiced precision. She knows which boards groan, which tones mean danger, which silences mean worse. Every day becomes an act of invisibility.

Echo Guard stays close, sometimes a shimmer in the mirror, sometimes a cool breath at her back. Their glow is sharper now, forged by purpose. They are not just protecting her anymore. They are building something new.

It begins with a whisper.

A voice inside that sounds like her, but is not.

"I can take this part," it says.

At first she thinks she imagined it. But when the shouting starts again, that voice steps forward, calm and focused. The world slows. She drifts behind her own eyes.

Echo Guard doesn't stop it. They guide through it. They know she needs help only one of the Echoes can give.

When it's over, the child shakes, but the pain feels far away. The new voice doesn't cry. It only breathes, steady and cold, holding the memory like a stone.

When I was little, I thought the small voice that told me right from wrong was Jiminy Cricket. He sat on my shoulder in my imagination, wagging a tiny finger and whispering, Be good and do as you're told! I believed everyone had one of those.

The first time the voice answered back with words that didn't sound like mine, I froze. It wasn't angry or loud, only steady, low, and certain.

"Breathe," it said.

I thought maybe my conscience had grown up with me.

But something about the way it spoke made a small tremor run through me. It felt older than me, calmer than me, more patient than anything I had ever known. I remember sitting perfectly still, waiting for it to happen again, listening for the soft stir of presence that meant I was not imagining things.

When it did return, it came with a quiet confidence that made the world feel less sharp at the edges.

Now, when I close my eyes, I find myself at the Ravenmarked Oak. This is my safe space.

It stands beside a narrow creek somewhere deep in the wilderness of my inner world, its branches leaning inward as if curious about the conversations beneath them. A raven is carved into the bark. A tire swing hangs from one heavy branch. A carved wooden bench rests beneath the tree, and around it grows a blanket of soft violet flowers that move gently in the wind.

This is where the echoes gather.

This is where I began to understand that the voices were not strangers. They were my internal family.

When I first arrived there, I didn't know their names. I only knew their feelings. One was steady as stone. One burned like hidden fire. One moved like static beneath the skin. One carried stillness the way the creek carried light.

"Who are you?" I remember asking into that quiet clearing.

A single voice answered, calm and grounded.

"The part that never sleeps."

Echo Guard.

At first, I thought I was losing my mind.

Then I realized I was finally meeting it.

Sometimes I think the Ravenmarked Oak had always been there, waiting for me to notice. Maybe it is where all the parts of me went when the world outside grew too loud. Maybe it is where they learned to keep watch, to carry the pieces I couldn't hold.

I didn't understand it then, but I felt it. Even before I knew the word survival, they were already practicing it for me.

The first few times I sensed them, it was like catching movement at the edge of vision, a shimmer, a sense that someone had just left but the air still remembered them. I would shake my head and tell myself it was imagination, but imagination doesn't answer back. Not like that. Not with intention.

When I finally listened, the fear didn't disappear, but it did soften. I started to understand that hearing them was not madness. It was communication. A kind of inner translation between danger and endurance.

They weren't strangers breaking in.

They were family knocking from the inside.

"You made us," Echo Guard said once, their voice calm and certain. *"We came from everything you survived."*

"Then why do I feel crazy?" I whispered.

"Because you are finally hearing what has always been said."

Those words wrapped around something aching inside me, soothing it without erasing it. It was the first time I understood that being whole doesn't mean being one. It means being many and still deserving to exist.

Back then, I couldn't name the other presences. I only knew that one burned like heat and another moved like still water. They stayed quiet, waiting for their time, watching the world through my eyes, measuring its dangers and deciding when to step forward.

Sometimes, during the day, I would feel a ripple inside me, a subtle shift, a tiny rearrangement of courage I didn't know I had. When I walked into a room that felt wrong, the fierce one would lift her chin. When I had to answer a question at school, the bright one would pull a smile onto my face even when it felt borrowed.

They were learning their roles by living inside my moments.

And I was learning that survival sometimes carries company.

Now, when I look back, I want to reach through time, take that girl's hand, and tell her, You are not broken for having many voices. You are extraordinary for finally listening to them.

I want to tell her she is not wrong or strange or destined for an ending written by someone else.

I want her to know she was building her own rescue long before anyone even considered rescuing her.

Even now, when life gets loud, I return to the Ravenmarked Oak. Sometimes we talk. Sometimes we sit in silence and wait for my heart to settle. I don't always understand the echoes, but I don't need to.

When I was younger, I knew something inside me worked differently, but I never had language for it. I only knew thoughts did not stay in a single lane. Sometimes they spoke back. Sometimes they felt borrowed. Sometimes they felt like remnants of a girl who existed before me.

Back then, the only stories I heard about voices were the kind that ended on the evening news. People said those voices made them dangerous, unstable, and broken. I promised myself I would never be like that.

Whatever lived in me was not evil. It wasn't loud. It was quiet and tired and trying to keep me safe.

But the fear still stuck.

I remember sitting on my bed at night, whispering to the dark, "Please don't let me be crazy."

I didn't know then that what I was really asking for was understanding, not silence. Just a little truth.

If someone had said the words Dissociative Identity Disorder to me then, I think I would have laughed or cried or run. I thought people with that diagnosis lived behind locked doors and barred windows. I didn't know that sometimes they were mothers who packed lunches, went to work, and smiled at their children. I didn't know that sometimes they were little girls sleeping beneath blankets that smelled of fear and detergent.

Echo Guard spoke quietly the first time I asked.

"Are we bad?" I whispered.

"No," they said. "We were born from bad things, but that isn't the same."

That conversation stayed with me. Later, when the diagnosis finally came, I remembered those words.

We were never the danger. We were the protection.

Another day, another whisper. This one softer, filled with a gentleness that should not have existed there.

"I will hold the good things," it said. "The sky. The warmth. The way sunlight feels."

So she let it.

Piece by piece, her world rearranged itself.

There was the one who hid. The one who smiled. The one who forgot. The one who watched.

And through it all, Echo Guard moved between them, quiet architect, guardian of the divide.

The house didn't notice, and the adults never saw it happening.

But inside, something vast was forming, a world built from fragments, safety stitched from fear.

At night, beneath the Ravenmarked Oak, Echo Guard stood at the center of it all, surrounded by faint presences, each one a self becoming possible. They did not mourn the splitting. They honored it. Because this was how she would live. How she would last.

The child slept at last, dreams crowded with whispers. They didn't try to fight for space or dominance. They simply began to exist.

And in the smallest corner of her dreaming, Echo Guard kept watch, steady and luminous, knowing the world had fractured, but the echo remained unbroken.

Little one,

I know this is the part where you start to disappear.

It doesn't happen all at once or in a way anyone else would notice. You still get up. You still answer when spoken to. But inside, something has already begun to change. You're learning how to leave without leaving. How to stay in the body just enough to survive while your mind runs somewhere safer.

I wish I could tell you that none of this is happening. I wish I could tell you the new house will be different. But I know better, and so do you. Even then, deep down, you know that danger doesn't care about the house. It follows you. It settles into voices. It learns the shape of fear and makes itself at home there.

What I need you to know is that the part of you that slips away isn't weak. The part of you that goes quiet isn't broken. She is saving you in the only way she knows how.

You are going to believe that disappearing means something is wrong with you. You'll think the drifting, and the distance, and the strange sense of being there and not there all at once. But the truth is the opposite. You were so real, so present to pain, that your mind had to create somewhere softer for you to rest.

The voices that start here, the steady one, the watchful one, the ones that feel like warmth and warning and company in the dark, they're not here to hurt you. They are born from love. Fierce love. Protective love. The kind of love a child should have received from the world around her, but instead had to grow inside herself.

You don't need to understand them yet. You only need to know that they're there.

You're not alone in that room. You aren't alone in that house.

I promise you that one day, when you are older and confused and trying to make sense of all of this, you will look back at the girl on that bed and realize she was never weak at all. She was building a way through.

I am so sorry for what you are carrying.

I am so proud of how you carry it.

And I promise, I will come back for you.

Love,
Me xxoo

The clearing beneath the Ravenmarked Oak is smaller tonight, not because the trees have moved closer, but because the air itself has compressed and thickened into something you could almost touch. The atmosphere presses down like a hand on the chest, heavy and insistent, making it harder to breathe.

The violet flowers at the oak's roots bend so low their petals touch the earth, trembling even though there is no wind. Some have begun folding inward completely, closing themselves against what's coming. The ground beneath them feels unstable, soft in places it shouldn't be, as if the earth itself is preparing to absorb something too heavy to hold on the surface.

The creek beyond the clearing runs faster now, its sound sharp and anxious, water rushing over stones with an urgency that wasn't there before. The temperature fluctuates wildly. One moment it's cool enough to raise goosebumps, the next warm and close and suffocating. The air tastes metallic, charged, like the moment before lightning strikes.

The raven in the branches above is no longer still. It shifts constantly from foot to foot, wings half spread, head turning sharply to track movement below. Its eyes are bright and watchful, and every few moments it releases a low guttural sound, not quite a cry, but a warning.

Echo Guard stands closest to the oak, both hands pressed flat against the carved raven in the trunk. Their posture is rigid, spine straight, shoulders pulled back. Their jaw is tight enough that the muscles in their neck stand out like cords. Their eyes scan the clearing in constant motion, the path, the shadows, the flowers, the creek, then back to the path again. They aren't just watching. They're calculating, assessing, preparing for impact. Their breathing is controlled but deliberate, each inhale measured and each exhale purposeful. They're bracing themselves and the others for what's about to break open.

Harmony kneels among the violet flowers, but her rocking has become more agitated now. Forward and back, forward and back, faster and more urgent. Her hands hover above the petals, fingers trembling.

She's trying to soothe something that hasn't arrived yet but she can already feel pressing against her chest. Her shoulders curve inward protectively and her breathing comes in shallow bursts. She knows. She can feel it in the way the flowers bend, in the way the earth has softened, in the way the air tastes like copper and fear.

Vex paces near the tire swing, but her movements have become sharper and more frantic. She doesn't walk. She stalks. Three steps forward, then a pivot so fast her feet skid slightly, then three steps back again. Her hands clench into fists, release, then clench again. She kicks at stones with more force than before, sending them scattering across the clearing with sharp cracks. The swing behind her sways wildly where she keeps brushing against it, the rope groaning.

She's all kinetic energy with nowhere to land, motion looking for purpose, restlessness that feels like a scream building in her throat.

Luna hovers near the edge of the clearing, her pale blue glow brighter than it has ever been, but flickering and pulsing like a candle flame in a draft. She wraps her arms around herself, small and fragile, and her light wavers with each breath.

She can feel what's coming. The betrayals. The hands. The isolation. The way trust will be weaponized. Her glow brightens for a moment, then dims, then brightens again, a heartbeat made of light and fear.

And Ember.

Ember stands where the path disappears into darkness, and the air around her no longer just shimmers. It distorts. Heat rises from her in visible waves that bend the light and make the trees behind her ripple and blur. Her outline flickers like she's being seen through flame. Her hands are clenched so tightly her whole body trembles with the effort of containment. Her breathing comes fast and ragged, each exhale sending pulses of heat into the cooling air.

She is no longer dormant potential.

She is changing.

"She's about to break," Harmony whispers, her voice tight with worry. "They're going to hurt her so badly."

"They already are," Echo Guard says quietly. Their hands press harder against the carved raven. "Every day. Every night. And no one is stopping it."

Vex kicks the base of the tire swing so hard it lurches sideways and the rope groans loudly.

"So what do we do?" she asks sharply. "Just watch? Just wait?"

"We prepare," Echo Guard says. Their jaw tightens further. "We get ready to hold her when she can't hold herself."

Ember's heat flares suddenly, bright and fierce. The violet flowers nearest to her curl at the edges, their petals browning.

"I want to burn it all down," she says, her voice cracking like splitting wood. All of it."

"You will," Echo Guard says quietly, eyes still fixed on the path. "When she needs you to."

Luna's glow flickers more violently.

"But it's going to hurt her," she whispers, tears running down her face. "The fire. The rage. It's going to hurt."

"Less than the silence will," Vex snaps. "Less than swallowing it."

Harmony's rocking intensifies.

"This is where everything changes," she says softly. "This is where she learns no one is coming to save her."

The clearing itself seems to respond. The ground beneath them shifts slightly and settles into something stronger and more stable. The oak's branches bend lower, forming a canopy that feels less like shelter and more like armor. The creek's rushing sound becomes steady and present, not peaceful, but watchful. The violet flowers begin glowing faintly in the dimming light, not with softness, but with defiance.

The raven above releases another low cry and spreads its wings fully, black feathers catching what little light remains.

Ember's heat builds higher. The air around her shimmers so violently now she's barely visible through the distortion. Her fists shake. Her breathing comes in sharp burning gasps.

"She's going to need me," Ember says. "When they sit him beside her at that table. When they lock her in that room. When the hands come in the dark. She's going to need someone who refuses to be quiet."

Echo Guard straightens further.

"Then we make sure you're ready."

Harmony looks up from the flowers, tears streaming.

"And we hold her through it. All of us."

Vex stops pacing long enough to meet their eyes.

"Together," she says.

Luna's glow steadies slightly.

"We don't let her disappear."

Above them, the raven settles its wings but keeps watching.

The clearing holds its breath.

The echoes stand closer together now, not touching, but near enough to feel each other's presence. Echo Guard steady and grounded. Harmony anxious but gentle. Vex sharp and ready. Luna is fragile but glowing.

And Ember burning.

Building.

Preparing to become the fire that will keep her alive.

The clearing transforms around them. It is no longer only a sanctuary. Now it is a fortress. Now it is a family gathering to protect what cannot protect itself.

The path ahead grows darker.

And in the darkness something is waiting.

But the echoes are waiting too.

And when the fire finally breaks free, they will be ready.

~IV~

The First Ghost

The dinner table was a stage, and I had learned all the wrong lines.

He sat at the head, fork in hand, eyes moving between his plate and my face with the kind of attention that made my stomach tighten. The questions always started small. Innocent. How was school? What did you learn today? Did you finish your homework?

But I could hear the sharpness beneath them, the way his voice tightened around certain words. His silence stretched too long when I answered. It was intimidating when he leaned forward, waiting for me to say the wrong thing.

I kept my eyes on my plate. I gently pushed peas around with my fork. Trying to make myself smaller.

*"Breathe,"*Echo Guard whispered, steady and low. *"Count the seconds between his questions. You know how this works."*

I did know. I had learned to read the weather of his moods the way sailors read storms,by the shift in air pressure, the way light changed before the sky opened up. But knowing didn't make me safe. It only made me vigilant.

"Are you listening to me?"

His voice cut through the quiet, and I flinched before I could stop myself.

"Yes," I said quickly. Too quickly.

He smiled, but it didn't reach his eyes. "Good. Because I asked you a question."

I hadn't heard it. I had been somewhere else,somewhere safer, somewhere his voice couldn't follow. But I couldn't tell him that. So I nodded and said, "Sorry. I was thinking."

"About what?"

The trap closed around the question. There was no right answer. If I said nothing, I was lying. If I told the truth, I was disrespectful. If I stayed silent, I was defiant.

"*Stay still,*" Echo Guard murmured. "*Let him talk. Don't give him anything to hold onto.*"

I swallowed and said, "Just school stuff."

He watched me for a long moment, then went back to his plate. But the tension didn't leave. It never did. He would keep grilling me until I would cry. Crying never helped, it just seemed to entertain him. His face had a look of satisfaction. Eventually I would take a few hits from him before being sent to my room to write lines or work on school work and learn something new.

I was twelve the first time I can remember, I tried to tell someone about how I was treated at home.

The guidance counselor had kind eyes and a soft voice, and when she asked if everything was okay at home, something inside me cracked open. I told her about the yelling. About the way he looked at me sometimes. About the fear that lived in my chest like a stone I couldn't swallow. I showed her the bruises on my arms and back.

She listened. She nodded. She looked and she said she believed me.

And then the Children's Aid Society came to the school.

They pulled me out of class and brought me to a small room with beige walls and a table that felt too big. I sat in a plastic chair, hands folded in my lap, heart pounding so hard I thought they could hear it.

I was mortified when I saw him walk in.

My stepfather. The man I had just reported. The man whose anger I had finally named out loud.

He sat down beside me, and the caseworker across from me, and I understood at that moment that no one was coming to save me.

I don't know why my mother wasn't there. I have asked myself that question a thousand times, turned it over in my mind like a stone worn smooth by water. She should have been there. She should have been the one sitting beside me, the one holding my hand, the one standing between me and the man I was afraid of.

But she wasn't. I don't know if she really ever knew what was happening.

And so I sat alone in that room with my abuser and a stranger who asked me questions I could no longer answer honestly. Because how could I? How could I tell the truth when the person I was afraid of was sitting right there, watching me, his face calm and concerned, his voice steady as he explained that I was confused, that I was struggling, that I had always been a difficult child?

The caseworker nodded. Took notes. Asked if I felt safe.

I looked at him. Then at her. Then at my hands.

"Yes," I whispered.

The file closed two weeks later.

At school, I became a liar. The girl who made things up for attention. The girl who couldn't be trusted. Teachers looked at me differently. Classmates whispered. And I learned that reaching out for safety could make you less safe than staying silent ever did.

"*They didn't see*," Echo Guard said quietly, a presence pressing close. "*But I did. I see you.*"

Something inside me had shifted, that I wasn't entirely alone even when the world decided I was.

Home had its own system of punishment. It began when I was six.

The first time it happened I didn't understand what was happening. He sat me at the kitchen table with a stack of lined paper and a pen. His voice was calm, almost pleasant, like this was something normal that happened in every house.

"You are going to write something for me," he said.

He told me to write the sentence *I will not disobey* one thousand times.

My hand cramped before I reached the first hundred lines. My fingers ached and my wrist burned, but I kept writing because I didn't know what would happen if I stopped. The house was quiet in the way quiet sometimes means something is waiting. I finished hours later and handed the pages to him carefully, hoping that being finished would be enough.

It wasn't ever enough. He would scrutinize to look for an error.

He checked every line and found three where my handwriting had become uneven.

"Start over," he said.

I looked up at him. My eyes burned but I already knew better than to cry.

"But I already finished." I said very meekly.

The belt came off so fast I didn't see it move. I only heard the sound and felt the sting across my legs.

"Start over."

"Don't cry," Echo Guard whispered quietly. *"Don't give him that. Just write."*

So I wrote again.

The lines didn't happen only once. They became something regular. Sometimes weekly. Sometimes more often. There was always a reason, whether it was talking back, moving too slow, not finishing my chores quick enough, looking at him wrong. Sometimes I felt myself just existing irritated him. The sentences changed but the lesson stayed the same.

Write until your hand hurts.

Write until you stop asking questions.

Write until silence feels safer than speaking.

Sometimes it was five thousand lines or more, he would add onto them all the time. Once it was seven thousand. That time I wrote for three days with my hand shaking so badly I could barely hold the pen. My shoulders ached from sitting in the same chair and my vision blurred across the page, but I kept writing because the alternative was worse.

He never explained the alternative. He didn't have to.

I understood the choice I was being given every time the paper appeared in front of me. Write, or face what happened later when the house became quiet. Write, or let his hands decide what happened next. Write until the words stopped feeling like language and became something closer to survival.

So I chose the line, every time.

"Keep going," Echo Guard said steadily. *"You can survive this. Just keep writing."*

But another voice was beginning to grow beneath Theirs. It was quieter at first, then sharper each time the pen touched the page again.

"This isn't fair," she whispered.

I didn't know her name yet.

I only knew the heat that followed her voice.

I would feel it spread through my chest each time he pointed at the page of my lines and ask what the sentence meant. I had to answer him. I had to explain the words I had already written thousands of times as if I were proving something instead of surviving something. Sometimes my mind was too tired to think clearly and sometimes fear made the meaning disappear before I could speak.

"I don't know," I would whisper.

"Then you didn't learn anything."

The belt again.

"Five thousand more. And this time you will explain every single one."

The rage had nowhere to go. I couldn't scream. I couldn't throw the pen. I couldn't tell him what I was thinking because that would only make it worse. So the fire stayed inside me, building slowly while I sat there with perfect posture and wrote the same sentence over and over until the words stopped meaning anything at all.

"I'm here," the burning voice said quietly. *"You don't have to carry this alone."*

And somewhere softer than both of them another presence stayed close enough for me to feel but not yet understand.

"Breathe," the whisper said. *"You can handle this."*

I hadn't met them all yet. I didn't understand that my mind was building something to help me survive what I couldn't stop. I only knew that when I sat at that table with the pen in my hand and the silence pressing in around me, I wasn't completely alone.

The echoes were already there.

Waiting.

Holding what I couldn't, but that I needed help to carry.

School became another kind of cage. Being bullied seemed to change shapes and locations but in the end it was consistent for me.

I thought maybe there would be one place where someone would see me. One adult who would notice. One moment where I could be safe.

But there wasn't.

The bus ride to school started every morning. I'd climb on and find a seat near the front, trying to make myself small, trying to disappear into the vinyl and metal. But they always found me.

The spit or gum would hit my hair first. Warm and wet. Then my shoulder. Then the back of my neck.

I didn't turn around. I learned early that turning around only made it worse. So I sat there, feeling it slide down my skin, feeling the laughter vibrate through the seats behind me, and I counted the stops until I could get off.

"Don't react," Echo Guard whispered. *"Stay still. Don't give them anything."*

But something hotter was building beneath my ribs.

"Tell them," another voice hissed, sharp and burning. *"Make them stop. Say something."*

I didn't know her name yet. I only knew the heat.

In class, they sang. A stupid song about fish heads that someone had turned into a taunt about my eyes. My eyes were too big, they said. Bug eyes. Fish eyes. Freak eyes.

"Fish heads, fish heads, roly poly fish heads..."

They'd sing it under their breath when the teacher wasn't looking. They'd sing it louder in the hallways. They'd sing it on the bus, in the cafeteria, during gym class when we were supposed to be running laps.

I tried to tell a teacher once. She looked at me like I was being dramatic.

"Kids tease," she said. "You need to grow thicker skin."

I didn't know how to explain that my skin was already so thick I could barely feel anything anymore. That I was holding so much inside that I didn't know how to behave like a normal kid. That I was reacting to things no child should ever have to carry.

I acted out. I know I did. I was angry and scared and I didn't know how to be anything else. I'd snap at teachers. I'd refuse to do schoolwork. I'd sit in the back of the class and stare at nothing until someone yelled at me to pay attention.

And when I defended myself, when I finally pushed back against the kids who wouldn't stop, I was the one sent to the hall.

Every….single….time.

I would try talking to the counselor when they sent me to the principal's office. I tried to explain that I wasn't trying to be difficult. That I was just so tired. That I didn't know how to make it stop.

But the words came out wrong. Or maybe they came out right and no one wanted to hear them.

Either way, nothing changed. I started feeling like a movie that when people got to some of the scenes, they would just cover their eyes. The scenes that no one wanted to watch. No one saw me, I knew that. What was hard was that it seemed no one wanted to.

One day, we were cleaning out our lockers. It was me and one other girl left in the hallway, both of us pulling out crumpled papers and forgotten textbooks.

She started throwing things at me.

Garbage from her locker. Balled up paper. An empty juice box. A broken pencil.

At first, I ignored it. I was good at ignoring things by then.

But she kept going. Laughing. Throwing. Aiming for my head.

The heat in my chest started to rise.

"Tell her to stop," the burning voice demanded. *"Make her stop."*

"Don't," Echo Guard said firmly. *"You'll get in trouble. You always get in trouble."*

"I don't care," the heat shot back. *"I'm tired of this."*

Another piece of garbage hit my shoulder.

And something inside me snapped.

I didn't think. I just moved. My foot connected with my math book and it went flying, spinning through the air in a perfect arc.

And then the sound of glass shattering.

The book had gone through the window.

Everything was suddenly completely silent. Just me and the broken glass and the girl staring at me with her mouth open.

Then the classroom door opened.

I was the only one brought to the office. The only one punished. The girl who'd been throwing things at me walked away without a word, without a consequence, without anyone even asking her what happened. Typical.

I tried to explain. Tried to say that she'd started it, that I'd only been defending myself.

But I was already the liar. The difficult one. The girl who couldn't be trusted.

I wasn't normally even allowed in the hallways. I was different. Already labelled a trouble maker.

So they sent me to the rubber room.

It was a 4x4 cement space, white and cold like the rest of the school. No window. No warmth. Just white walls that seemed to press in closer the longer I sat there.

The door locked from the outside.

I heard the click every time they closed it, and my chest would tighten with panic. What if there was a fire? What if something happened and I couldn't get out? What if they forgot I was in here?

Sometimes they brought me schoolwork. Most of the time, they didn't.

It was just me and a desk. No chair. So I'd stand, or I'd sit on the cold dirty carpet floor, and I'd wait.

I would sit in there for hours and hours. Most of the time that is where I spent most days all day.

No one checked on me. No one asked if I was okay. No one seemed to care that a twelve year old girl was locked in a room by herself with no way out.

The silence in that room was different from the silence at home. At home, the silence was full of waiting, full of fear about what might happen next.

Here, the silence was empty.

It was the sound of no one caring. No one listening. No one coming.

So I talked to the voices.

I didn't know they were echoes yet. I thought they were imaginary friends, the kind of thing kids were supposed to grow out of. I thought maybe I was crazy for still hearing them, for still needing them.

But they were all I had.

"I'm here," Echo Guard would say, steady and calm. *"You're not alone."*

"This isn't fair," the burning voice would hiss. *"None of this is fair."*

"I know," I'd whisper back, my voice barely audible in the empty room. "I know."

The echoes became more real in that room. More necessary. They were the only ones who witnessed what was happening to me. The only ones who believed me. The only ones who stayed.

I spent so many days in that room that I lost count. The white walls blurred together. The hours stretched and contracted until time didn't mean anything anymore.

And I understood something I hadn't fully understood before.

There was nowhere safe.

Not at home, where my stepfather's anger waited like a storm I couldn't predict.

Not at school, where I was spit on and mocked and punished for defending myself.

Not in the system, where adults asked questions they didn't want answered and locked me in rooms when I became inconvenient.

There was no sanctuary. No adult who saw me. No place where I could actually rest.

Just the rubber room. Just the cold cement. Just the locked door and the fear of fire. The voices in my head became the only help I had left.

"We're still here," Echo Guard said one day, her presence pressing close in the silence.

"We're not leaving," the burning voice added, fierce and hot.

And I believed them because they were all I had.

The only witnesses. The only ones who cared. The only proof that I wasn't disappearing completely.

I sat on that cold floor, my back against the white wall, and I talked to the voices that everyone said weren't real. And they talked back. When they spoke to me it meant that for a little while, in that terrible room, I wasn't completely alone.

I would like to say that other than home and school there was somewhere I should have also felt safe. I went to church every Sunday. I went to church with my mom and stepfather and the kids in the congregation were the ones that bullied me at school.

They had told their parents all about the weird girl that they had to lock in a room at school because she was so bad.

The church smelled like old wood and dust, the kind of smell that clings to the back of your throat. The ceiling peaked high above us, and light filtered through stained glass in fractured colors that didn't quite reach the scratchy blue carpet beneath my feet.

I sat in the pew, sucking on my bottom lip, tasting metal.

The door had slammed on my fingers that morning. Accidentally, he said. But I had seen his face in the moment before it happened, the flicker of something cold and deliberate. And now my lip was fat and split up no matter how many times I tried to stop it bleeding it just would start again.

The pastor stood at the front, talking about blessings and gratitude, and my stepfather sat beside me with his hands folded, nodding along like he hadn't just hurt me hours before.

After the service, the pastor was shaking hands with the congregation as we left the church. His hand was heavy on my shoulder, his smile wide and warm.

"You're so lucky," he said, his voice booming in the quiet hallway. "Do you know how lucky you are?"

I blinked up at him, confused. My lip throbbed. My fingers ached.

"Your father," he continued, gesturing toward my stepfather, who stood a few feet away, talking to another parishioner. "He didn't have to adopt you. He chose you. He chose to love you. That's a gift, you know. Not every child gets that."

I nodded because I didn't know what else to do. Feeling my tongue on my swollen lip and my fingers throbbing.

He kept talking. About sacrifice. About grace. About how blessed I was to have a man like that in my life. The words piled on top of each other, heavy and suffocating. I couldn't believe he couldn't see it!

I knew I hadn't slammed my own fingers in the door. I knew the split in my lip wasn't an accident. But here was this man,this pastor, this adult, this person everyone respected,telling me how lucky I was.

And I started to wonder if I was wrong. If maybe I had imagined it. What if maybe I was the problem all along?

"You're not," a voice whispered, softer than Echo Guard. Gentler. *"You're not wrong. You're not the problem."*

I didn't know her name yet either. But I felt her there, a warmth pressing against the cold doubt, a hand steadying me when my own legs wanted to give out.

The pastor finally stopped talking, patted my shoulder one more time, and walked away.

I stood there on the scratchy burgundy carpet, surrounded by the smell of old wood and the light filtering through stained glass, and I quietly questioned my sanity and my perception.

Somewhere deep inside, beneath the doubt and the shame and the fear, something refused to let go of the truth.

At night, I dressed in oversized t-shirts and baggy jeans. I kept my hair short. I avoided anything that might make me look feminine, anything that might draw attention to the fact that my body was changing in ways I couldn't control.

I was trying to protect myself the only way I knew how, by disappearing into shapelessness, by refusing to be seen as anything other than a child. Because I understood, even then, that my body was being weaponized against me. That being perceived as attractive was dangerous.

So I made myself small. I made myself invisible. Made myself into something that couldn't be wanted.

But it didn't make a difference because at night, he would come to my room regardless.

I would hear the movement first, the creak of floorboards, the shift of air, the presence that didn't belong. I would lie very still, eyes closed, pretending to be asleep, hoping that if I didn't move, didn't breathe too loud, didn't acknowledge what was happening, maybe it wouldn't be real.

But it was real.

What happened there lived in my body before it lived in my words. It lived in the way my skin crawled when I heard footsteps in the hallway. It lived in the way I flinched at touch, even kind touch, even safe touch. It lived in the cold sheets and the dark room and the shadow that crossed my doorway when everyone else was asleep.

By the time I had words for it, everyone had already decided I was a liar.

So I stayed silent.

And the echoes learned to speak for me.

"Look at the ceiling," Echo Guard said, their voice cutting through the dark. *"Count the cracks. There are seven. Focus on them."*

I did. I traced them with my eyes, followed the lines from one end of the room to the other.

"Breathe," they continued. *"Let's go somewhere safe, take a deep breath"*

I breathed.

"You're not here," another voice whispered, softer and warmer. *"You're somewhere else. Somewhere safe."*

I didn't know where that was. But I tried to imagine it. I tried to pull myself out of my body and into some other place where hands couldn't reach me, where shame couldn't follow.

"We've got you," a third voice murmured, restless and sharp. *"We're not leaving. We're right here."*

The voices layered over each other, creating a kind of distance between me and what was happening. They pulled me apart just enough that I wasn't entirely present, wasn't entirely aware. They held the pieces of me that couldn't hold themselves.

And when it was over, when the shadow finally left and the door closed and the house settled back into silence, I lay there staring at the ceiling, counting cracks, breathing in and out, and feeling the echoes hum quietly around me like a shield I didn't know I had built.

I didn't understand yet that my mind was learning how to survive by splitting the weight across many shoulders. I didn't understand that dissociation wasn't a failure, it was a strategy. A way of staying alive when staying whole would have broken me.

All I knew was that I wasn't alone.

Even when I should have been.

The dinner table again.

His voice, asking another question. My hands, gripping my fork too tight. The air, thick with the weight of everything unsaid.

But this time, something was different.

This time, there was heat.

It started low in my chest, a flicker of warmth that grew hotter with every word he spoke. It spread through my ribs, up my throat, into my jaw. My teeth clenched. My breath came faster.

"Steady," Echo Guard warned. *"Don't let him see."*

But the heat didn't listen. It kept building, kept rising, kept pushing against the walls I had built to keep it contained.

And then it spoke.

"Enough."

The word was sharp and burning, and it didn't come from me. It came from somewhere deeper, somewhere I hadn't known existed until that moment.

"Enough," the voice said again, louder this time. *"He doesn't get to do this anymore."*

I felt her then, fully, completely. Not just a whisper or a presence, but a voice with weight and fire and refusal.

"I'm here," she said, and the heat in my chest flared brighter. *"And I'm not going anywhere."*

My stepfather was still talking, still asking questions, still waiting for me to stumble. But I wasn't listening anymore. I was listening to her.

"You don't have to be afraid," she said. *"I'll carry the anger. I'll hold the fire. You just have to let me."* And I did.

I let the heat rise. Let it fill the space where fear used to live. Let it burn through the shame and the doubt and the silence.

I didn't say anything out loud. I didn't have to. Because she was there now, standing between me and him, a wall of fire that he couldn't see but I could feel.

"My name is Ember," she said. *"And I'm not letting him hurt you anymore."* Around her, I felt the others stirring. The steady one who had been there all along. The soft one who whispered comfort. The restless one who kept moving. The tender one who still believed in something good.

They were waking up. All of them. Gathering around me like a family I didn't know I had built.

And for the first time, I understood: I wasn't breaking.

I was becoming something necessary.

Later, when the dinner was over and the dishes were cleared and I was alone in my room, I sat on the edge of my bed and felt them all there with me.

Echo Guard, steady and watchful. Ember, burning and fierce. And the others, still unnamed but present, their voices humming quietly in the background.

"We're not going anywhere," Echo Guard said.

"We're yours," Ember added. *"And you're ours."*

I didn't have words for what that meant yet. I didn't understand that my mind had learned to survive by creating a constellation of voices, each one carrying a different piece of what I couldn't carry alone.

But I felt it.

And I knew, somewhere deep and certain, that I wasn't alone anymore.

Not then.

Not ever again.

Little one,

This is the chapter where you begin to fear your own fire. For so long you believed survival meant being quiet.

I know that you learned to shrink yourself and soften your voice, hoping danger might pass over you if you made yourself small enough. You thought silence was helping you stay strong. You thought being obedient kept you safe. You believed if you endured long enough someone would finally see you and stop it.

But something inside you has reached its limit now. The anger rising in your chest feels frightening because no one ever told you that anger can be sacred. No one told you that sometimes anger is simply the sound of a boundary finally waking up. You will one day learn to control your anger but that will only come when you understand.

Ember didn't arrive to destroy you. She arrived to protect the parts of you that silence could no longer carry.

When that heat rose inside you and the room went still, you thought you had become something dangerous. What was really happening was that you were refusing to disappear. One day you will understand that Ember was never your enemy. She was your shield. She was the voice that said no when the rest of you had been forced to say nothing.

I wish I could sit beside you in that small room and hold your shaking hands and tell you that none of this makes you broken. You are building something inside yourself that will one day save your life. One day you will understand the echoes. One day you will thank the fire. Until then, hold on. I am proud of the courage it took to feel what you felt.

Love,
Me xxoo

The clearing beneath the Ravenmarked Oak is restless tonight.

Not just moving. Restless and agitated. The air itself feels wrong, too thick to breathe properly, pressing down on everything like a hand over a mouth. The flowers at the oak's roots are wilting, their petals curling inward and trembling with a violence that has nothing to do with wind. Some have already fallen, scattered across the ground like small purple bruises.

The earth beneath them is unstable, soft in places it should be solid, shifting slightly with each step as if the ground itself isn't sure it can hold what's coming. Small cracks have appeared near the oak's roots, thin fractures spreading outward like veins.

The creek beyond the clearing runs fast and anxious, water rushing over stones with a sound that feels almost frantic. It's not the steady flow of earlier interludes, but something urgent, something trying to outrun itself. The temperature swings wildly. One moment the air feels suffocatingly warm, the next cold enough to raise goosebumps. It tastes metallic and sharp, like the moment before a storm breaks.

The raven in the branches above isn't watching calmly anymore. It shifts constantly, wings half spread, head jerking from side to side. Every few moments it releases a sharp cry, not a warning this time, but something closer to alarm.

Echo Guard stands at the base of the oak, both hands pressed flat against the trunk on either side of the carved raven. His posture is rigid, spine straight, feet planted wide. His jaw is clenched tightly enough that the muscles in his neck stand out like cables. His breathing is controlled but heavy, each inhale deliberate and each exhale measured. His eyes scan the clearing in constant motion, the path, the flowers, the creek, then back to the path again.

He isn't just watching anymore.

He's preparing.

"She's going to run," he says quietly, his voice low and certain.

Ember paces near the edge of the clearing, but her fire has changed. It isn't the wild protective rage from before. It's sharper now, more focused, heat that propels instead of consumes. Her movements are quick and purposeful along the tree line. Her breathing comes fast and heavy. The air around her shimmers with urgency rather than fury.

She stops suddenly.

"Good," she says. "She needs to move. She needs to get out."

"She needs to survive," Echo Guard corrects, still watching the path.

"Same thing," Ember answers, resuming her pacing.

The heat radiating from her pulses with each step.

By the creek, Harmony kneels among the wilting flowers, but her presence is dimmer now. Fading. Her outline looks less solid, as if she's already beginning to disappear. She rocks forward and back slowly, weaker with each movement. Her hands hover above the dying petals, trembling.

"I won't be able to reach her," she whispers. "Not where she's going."

Vex is everywhere at once.

She doesn't pace. She runs.

Short bursts of motion that start and stop without pattern. Three steps toward the tire swing, pivot, then a sprint toward the creek.

She stops, turns, runs back to the oak. Her hands flex and release again and again. She kicks stones, roots, anything in her path. The swing behind her sways wildly each time she collides with it. Her whole body vibrates with kinetic energy that has nowhere to land.

"She's going to shatter," Vex says breathlessly. "Completely. Not like before. Worse."

"I know," Echo Guard answers.

"And we're just going to let her?"

"We're going to hold her through it."

Vex freezes for half a second, chest heaving.

"How? If she breaks into pieces, how do we…"

"We become the pieces," Echo Guard says calmly. "We carry what she can't carry."

Luna stands near the shadows at the edge of the clearing, her pale blue glow subdued, barely brighter than moonlight. She wraps her arms around herself, small and fragile, watching the path with wide eyes. Her light doesn't flicker. It simply holds.

"It's going to hurt her," Luna says softly.

"Yes," Echo Guard answers.

"And us."

"Yes."

The clearing responds to their gathering tension. The oak's branches creak and bend lower as if trying to create shelter, though the movement feels strained and uncertain. The flowers continue to wilt and their violet glow dims almost completely. The ground shifts again beneath their feet.

Harmony stops rocking.

She lifts her head slowly.

"I'm going to disappear," she says quietly.

It isn't a question.

Echo Guard finally turns toward her.

"For a while."

"How long?"

"As long as it takes."

Ember stops pacing and faces the others. Her heat flares once, bright and sharp.

"She's going to run tonight," she says. "Under bridges. Into darkness. With people who don't care if she lives or dies."

"I know."

"And we're going to let her."

"We're going to go with her."

Vex begins running again, tight circles now, restless and sharp.

"This is different," she says. "This isn't hiding. This isn't going quiet. This is…"

"Shattering," Harmony finishes softly. "Complete dissociation."

The raven above releases another sharp cry. The creek grows louder. The temperature drops suddenly, then rises again with Ember's heat.

Echo Guard presses his hands harder against the oak.

"When she runs," he says, his voice steady across the clearing, "she's going to lose hours. Maybe days. She won't remember where she goes or what she does. She'll come back to herself bleeding and confused."

"And we'll be there," Ember says.

"All of us," Echo Guard answers. "Scattered. Fragmented. But there."

Luna's glow brightens slightly.

"Will she know we're with her?"

"No," Echo Guard says. "Not consciously. But she'll feel us. The way she always has."

Vex finally stops moving. Her body trembles with contained energy.

"And after?" she asks. "When she comes back?"

Echo Guard looks toward the dark path beyond the clearing.

"Someone new will be waiting."

Harmony lifts her head.

"Harmony," she whispers, speaking her own name like a goodbye.

"Yes," Echo Guard says gently. "You'll arrive in the quiet after the chaos. When she finally stops running long enough to breathe."

The clearing holds its breath.

The flowers bend low against the cracked earth. The creek rushes louder. The oak's branches groan under invisible weight.

Ember's fire sharpens to a single point of heat.

"She's going to survive this," she says.

"She is," Echo Guard answers.

"Because we won't let her disappear."

"No," Echo Guard says quietly. "We'll become the map that leads her back."

Vex begins moving again, slower now and more deliberate.

"Then we get ready."

Luna's glow steadies.

"We stay close."

Harmony's outline grows faint.

"Even when she can't feel us."

The raven spreads its wings fully, black feathers catching what little light remains. The clearing trembles once more beneath them.

Echo Guard straightens and pulls his hands away from the oak.

"She's about to run," he says softly.

"And when she does…"

"We run with her," Ember answers.

The echoes stand together in the restless clearing, not touching but close enough to feel each other's presence. The air presses down. The flowers wilt. The creek rushes anxiously toward something none of them can see.

On the path beyond the oak, in the darkness just past the clearing's edge, footsteps begin.

Fast.

Heavy.

Running.

The echoes don't move to stop her.

They gather themselves instead.

Because this isn't the moment for protection.

This is the moment for witness.

For holding what can't be held whole.

For becoming the pieces that will one day learn to speak in harmony.

The girl runs past the clearing without seeing it.

And the echoes,

all five of them,

follow her into the dark.

~V~

The First Shatter

I remember the sound before the pain, the tile against my skin and the air pulled tight in my throat. For years I called that night chaos, but now I understand it was the beginning of my own voice learning how to move.

"You still shake when you talk about it," the adult voice inside me says softly.

I nod toward her memory. I didn't think we would survive.

The floor steadied me when nothing else could. It was cold on my feet. I curled small with my forehead pressed to my knees and counted my breaths the way I had learned in places where crying was not safe, in and out.

There is a point when the body decides what it is going to do before the mind can. It isn't courage yet it is brave. An emotion necessary for survival.

That is when I felt him, not as a voice and not even as a thought, but as a shift inside the panic, a stillness spreading through the noise. I used to think those moments were luck, the body saving itself. Now I understand he had been there longer than I knew.

Echo Guard.

He didn't arrive that night. He stepped forward from where he had always been. His calm moved through me like the hush before snowfall and fear loosened its grip just enough for breath to return.

"It wasn't madness," the older voice says gently. "It was protection."

Back then I only knew the sound of my heartbeat, the wall behind me, and the voice outside the door. I was trapped between porcelain and plaster with my arms over my head and the air thick with fear. I was trying to block the tirade of blows from my stepfather.

Echo Guard steadied the shaking, but another current stirred beneath his calm, hot and restless and impossible to ignore. The two forces moved around each other inside me like weather learning a new pattern. Echo Guard didn't try to stop the heat. He anchored it, giving it shape instead of letting it burn through everything.

The feeling of being trapped intensified as I was stuck. Stuck between the tub and the toilet waiting for the fury of his fists to tire.

Ember moved forward against that boundary.

"Let her move!."

"She will."

Their voices were not arguments. They were agreements, two protectors learning how to guard the same life in different ways.

Ember didn't ask permission. She claimed the moment.

I was on my feet with an uppercut I had learned in Tae Kwon Do. I reacted before thought caught up with me and the fear made me retreat. Motion came first, and then heat followed. I remember the shock on his face, the distance that opened between us, then the hallway, the door, and out in the cold night. I remember that night as I ran out of the house was one of the few nights I remember my mom being there. I remember her grabbing him by his legs to give me more time to get out of the house.

The air outside hit like water.I ran until my lungs burned and the house disappeared behind me. I had no shoes or jacket but something inside didn't care. When I finally looked back, a small smile touched my mouth.

I still don't know whose smile it was.

Ember's fierce relief. Echo Guard's quiet pride. Or my own self finally breaking free.

"You thought that smile was wrong," the older voice says.

"It felt powerful," I answered.

It was the first time power belonged to us.

That night I learned freedom doesn't always arrive gently. Sometimes it arrives when it's earned by making difficult choices.

After that I drifted toward other kids who lived on the edge. We were runaways and dropouts and half believers in our own survival. We shared cigarettes and stories at the playgrounds beneath the lights that flickered like warnings. I remember the laughter that never reached our eyes and the bottle passed around like communion. We called ourselves friends, but really we were strays circling the same hunger, for safety and for somewhere to land.

"You were searching for a home," the older voice reminds me.

"I wanted the kind from television," I answer quietly. "The kind where the parents talk to their kids and hug them. The ones where the parents are focused on safety and comfort."

When the nights stretched too long I built stories. I played every role inside them, the hero, the rescuer, the girl who was chosen. Maybe Ember and Echo Guard were already there, hidden inside those characters, helping me build adventures strong enough to hold what the real world could not.

Sometimes I sat alone on a playground swing and imagined someone walking toward me, someone who knew how to hold softness and truth at the same time. I created conversations in my head, whole scenes that felt safer than the life I was living.

"You aren't alone," the stories whispered.

One night beneath a bridge with the river moving quietly beside me, something changed. This was no longer pretending. This was my life, the park benches, the borrowed blankets, the wandering.

And somehow that truth didn't crush me. Somehow it actually steadied me..

Echo Guard remained steady beneath my ribs. Ember stayed warm in my hands. For the first time they weren't pulling in opposite directions. They moved around something new, a stillness that arrived as a breath, soft and steady.

Not silence….not fire, but something balanced.

I didn't know her name yet. I only recognized the feeling, the space where heat and vigilance could rest without disappearing.

Harmony.

She didn't speak. She didn't need to. She was simply there.

Her presence changed the rhythm between the others. Ember softened from flame to warmth. Echo Guard relaxed by a single breath. Even Vex, somewhere along the restless edges of my thoughts, grew quiet.

Harmony didn't take control. Instead, she created some space.

Inside that space something unfamiliar appeared. Not total peace but a kind of peace.

It wasn't permanent and it wasn't complete, but it was real enough that I noticed the difference.

"That was the first time peace didn't scare you," the older voice says.

"It didn't feel like emptiness anymore," I answered. "It felt like belonging."

I leaned back against the concrete and watched the sky change slowly from black to blue. The world was still uncertain, but something inside me had shifted.

Echo Guard watched. Ember remained warm. Harmony breathed between them.

I didn't have a home yet.

But for the first time, I felt like I carried one within me.

When I look back now I see a girl learning to recognize her own strength. I see fragments that refused to disappear. I see that the moment I thought I had shattered was the moment something inside me began to gather itself.

The silence inside me didn't ache anymore.

And somewhere I understood something I had never known before. I wasn't only surviving. I was growing and this was a new start.

Little one,

You're realizing we're different. You did this because you had too. I'm starting to understand a little more that you survived so I could thrive.

Thank you!

I know you believed survival meant not moving and making yourself small. You learned to shrink, to endure, to wait for the storm to pass. You thought bravery meant holding your breath until danger moved on.

But that night something different happened.

You didn't run because you were weak. You ran because your body finally remembered that it deserved to live.

I know you were confused by the smile that came afterward. It felt wrong to feel powerful when everything around you had been built to make you small. Power had always belonged to someone else. Power had always meant danger.

But that smile was not cruelty, it was recognition.

A part of you realized that you were not completely trapped. You started to see a way to survive.

Echo Guard steadied your breath when panic tried to swallow you. Ember pushed you forward when fear tried to freeze you. And somewhere in that cold night air, another presence began to form, quiet and patient.

Harmony. She arrived not with fire or force, but with patience. With the gentle reminder that your mind could be more than a battlefield. That there could be a place inside you where all the pieces could rest.

I know you didn't understand and you felt like it was a collapse.

You were learning that something inside you were seeing all the wrongs you have had to endure.

You believed you were lost during those nights under the playground lights. You thought you were drifting farther away from the life you were supposed to have, but what you were really doing was building something.

You were learning that home doesn't always come from walls or families or places that promise safety.

Sometimes home grows slowly inside the spaces you protect within yourself.

Inside your courage. Inside the echoes that refused to abandon you.

One day you will look back on that night not as the moment you shattered, but as the moment you cracked open enough for something stronger to grow.

You were not breaking. You were growing, and even when you felt alone beneath bridges and streetlights, you never truly were.

Echo Guard watched.

Ember burned.

Harmony waited.

And I was always here, becoming you.

I am proud of the girl who ran toward life even when she thought she was running away. I'm sorry for the way it was easier to blame you than anyone else.

Love,
Me xxoo

The clearing beneath the Ravenmarked Oak is different tonight.

Not smaller. Not restless. Not compressed with anxiety or thick with warning.

Different.

The air is warmer now, genuinely warm, the kind of warmth that touches skin and stays there, gentle and welcoming. The violet flowers at the oak's roots are no longer wilting or trembling. They glow with softer light, their purple petals edged with gold, as if the sun has found a way to reach them even in twilight. Some have lifted their faces upward, opening instead of curling inward.

The ground beneath them is solid and steady. No cracks. No shifting uncertainty. Just earth that holds without question.

The creek beyond the clearing flows differently too. It isn't rushing with frantic energy. It moves like breathing now, steady and rhythmic. The sound of water over stone is almost musical, a gentle pulse that fills the space without overwhelming it. The temperature has risen enough that the cold edge is gone, replaced by something that feels almost like an embrace.

The tire swing hangs visible and inviting, swaying slightly in a breeze that carries the scent of growing things instead of decay. The carved bench beneath the oak looks less like a place to collapse and more like a place to rest. To sit. To stay.

Everything feels illuminated. Not harshly, but clearly. As if the clearing itself has decided to stop hiding.

Echo Guard stands at the base of the oak, but his posture has changed entirely.

His hands rest gently against the trunk on either side of the carved raven, not pressing, not gripping, just touching. His shoulders have dropped. The rigid tension that held his spine straight for so long has softened. He breathes deeply and slowly, as if testing whether the air will hold him. His eyes are still watchful, still scanning the clearing, but something has shifted in his gaze now.

Not vigilance born of fear.

Vigilance born of care.

"She's going to see something beautiful," he says quietly, his voice carrying wonder instead of warning.

Ember sits closer to the others than she ever has before.

Not pacing. Not burning with sharp protective heat. She's settled near the base of the oak, her fire changed entirely, golden now, warm instead of white hot. The air around her shimmers gently like sunlight on water. She watches the glowing flowers with something that looks almost like tenderness.

"It's moving toward something beautiful," she says softly. "Not away from danger. Toward light."

She reaches out and touches one of the violet flowers.

It doesn't wilt.

It glows brighter.

Harmony stands fully visible now, not dim, not fading, not hiding near the creek.

She is here.

Present.

Her outline is solid. Her voice is clear and strong. She moves among the flowers with gentle hands, touching petals and smoothing leaves. Her presence no longer cools the air. It warms it, filling the clearing with something that feels like hope made tangible.

"There is light here," she says, smiling. "Real light. Not just the absence of darkness, but actual warmth."

She kneels beside the creek and trails her fingers through the water. It catches the golden glow from the flowers and reflects it back, multiplying the light.

"She's going to remember this," Harmony continues. "She's going to hold this moment when everything else feels impossible."

Vex is still.

Not frozen.

Still.

Her restless energy has redirected entirely. She crouches near a cluster of flowers, studying the way the light moves across their petals. Her hands, usually clenched or flexing, are open and gentle. She touches a violet bloom carefully, watching how it responds to her presence.

"Look how it catches the light," she whispers, her voice filled with something close to awe. "It isn't running. It's just glowing."

She sits back on her heels and looks up into the oak's branches.

"I didn't know we could do this," she says. "I didn't know we could be still and it wouldn't hurt."

Luna arrives with full presence.

Her pale blue glow is bright now, not subdued and not hiding in shadows. She moves through the clearing like moonlight made solid, her light touching everything gently. She stands near the tire swing and pushes it once, watching it sway in the warm air.

"This is what we're surviving for," she says softly. "Not just to escape the dark. To reach moments like this."

She turns toward the others, her glow steady and hopeful.

"She's going to learn that love exists. That tenderness doesn't always betray. That beauty can be real without being dangerous."

The five echoes stand together now, not scattered and not competing for space, but gathered. Close enough to feel each other's presence. Close enough to speak without raising their voices.

Echo Guard's hands slide down from the oak trunk and rest at his sides.

"We can hold gentleness too," he says. "Not just danger. Not just survival. We can hold this."

Ember's golden fire pulses once, warm and steady.

"The chapter that's coming isn't about breaking," she says. "It's about remembering what didn't break."

Harmony moves to stand beside her.

"The horses," she says. "The mother. The brother. The Godfather. All the light that existed alongside the darkness."

Vex nods slowly.

"She needs to remember not everything was pain."

Luna's glow brightens.

"That love was real. That tenderness mattered. That she was seen and held and valued."

The clearing responds to them.

The flowers glow brighter, their golden edges spreading until the violet petals seem to hold sunlight. The creek's rhythm steadies into something that sounds almost like a lullaby. The oak's branches lift slightly, creating more space and more light. The tire swing sways in invitation.

Above them, the raven does something it has never done before.

It settles.

Not perching to watch.

Not preparing to warn.

Settling.

It tucks its wings close to its body and shifts its weight as if making itself comfortable, as if deciding to stay. Its black feathers catch the golden light from the flowers below, and for a moment it looks less like a sentinel and more like something that belongs.

Like home.

Echo Guard looks up at the raven and something in his expression softens completely.

"It isn't just watching anymore," he says.

"No," Harmony agrees. "It's staying."

The echoes stand together beneath the Ravenmarked Oak, and for the first time in any interlude, none of them are preparing for danger.

They're preparing for beauty.

For light.

For the memory of a mother's hand and a brother's eyes and a godfather's belief and horses that moved like grace made visible.

"She's going to need this," Echo Guard says quietly. "When the darkness comes back, and it will, she's going to need to remember this existed too."

Ember's fire warms the air around them all.

"Then we hold it for her," she says. "We hold the light the same way we hold the dark."

Vex touches another flower.

"We hold everything," she says. "That's what we do."

Luna's pale blue light mingles with Ember's golden warmth, creating something new that looks like dawn.

"We survive for this," she says. "For moments when tenderness is real. When love doesn't hurt. When beauty exists without conditions."

Harmony kneels and places both hands flat on the steady ground.

"This is what we were preparing for," she says. "Not just to endure. To live. To hold joy alongside grief. To remember that light exists even when we can't see it."

The clearing holds them all. Five echoes gathered beneath an ancient oak, surrounded by glowing flowers, beside a gentle creek, under a raven that has finally made its home.

The air is warm. The ground is steady. The light is real.

And on the path beyond the clearing, in the darkness that will soon give way to memory, a girl is about to step into an arena filled with white horses and her mother's quiet pride.

She doesn't know yet that this moment will become a lantern.

But the echoes know.

They stand together, not scattered but gathered, and they prepare to hold the light the same way they held the dark, with everything they have, with everything they are, together.

The raven settles deeper into its branch.

The flowers glow brighter.

And beneath the Ravenmarked Oak, the echoes finally understand,

This isn't just survival.

This is what they were surviving for.

~VI~

The First Disappearance

The noise inside me wasn't just chaos anymore. It had meaning. I didn't understand that yet. I only knew it felt heavier now, louder, shaped by something I couldn't name. Survival does that. It teaches the body to speak long before the mind is ready to hear.

I was seventeen when the house stopped being a home. Maybe it never had been, but there is something uniquely painful about realizing the people who are supposed to love you simply never learned how.

When my father told me to leave, it wasn't rage. It wasn't disappointment. It was something colder, it was indifference. I remember standing in the entryway, one hand on my bag, waiting for him to soften, to look up at me with even a flicker of hesitation. I waited for that moment every child prays for, the moment a parent realizes what they are losing. But he only sighed, long and tired, the way someone sighs when a commercial interrupts their favorite show.

"You need to figure your life out," he said, eyes on the floor. "I can't keep doing this. I love you but sometimes you need tough love."

Tough love? I couldn't understand this at all. Was there any other kind? That was all I ever had was tough love. To this day I always look back on this moment and remember something my Uncle said to me. "Children need discipline but they need hugs too."

He can't keep doing what? What part of having a daughter was too heavy for him to carry? This was where I came running for my life! He knew that but sadly I was still too much.

The silence that followed stretched across the entryway like something physical, something thick enough to press against my lungs. I stood there longer than I should have, waiting for the moment every child secretly believes will come, the moment when a parent realizes they have gone too far. I waited for him to look up, to soften, to see me. But nothing changed.

Behind my ribs, the echoes reacted before I did.

Ember burned first, heat rising through my chest like a match struck in a dark room.

"Say something," she hissed. *"Make him look at you."*

Vex leaned against the inside of my thoughts, amused in that sharp way she always was when pain arrived.

"Or don't," she said lightly. *"Watching him pretend you don't matter is almost entertaining."*

Echo Guard stepped between them, younger then, not yet the steady force he would become.

"Stop," he said quietly. *"She can't carry both of you right now."*

But they were already there. Already speaking. Already filling the space where my own voice had collapsed. And in that moment I understood something I had always feared, I wasn't just afraid of losing him. I was afraid he had already decided I wasn't worth keeping.

I wanted to ask, but the words dried in my throat. Silence rushed in. Ember stirred restlessly, heat gathering behind my ribs. Echo Guard hovered, steady but younger then, less patient, unsure how to stop the collapse inside me. Harmony was nowhere. Vex whispered lightly in the background, amused and bitter.

"Do you see," she murmured. *"He doesn't want you."*

My chest tightened.

"Stop," I whispered under my breath.

"Why? It's true," she answered. Her voice was bright and cutting, a shard of glass pretending to be a companion.

Ember's heat flared.

"Say it again and I will tear you apart," she snarled inside me.

Vex laughed.

"Fiery and cute. but she knows I'm right."

Echo Guard stepped forward, his voice low, young, and unsteady.

"Enough. I already told you she doesn't need this right now"

 I broke under the weight of it.

"I can't stay?" I asked him, my real voice so small I barely recognized it.

He looked at me and shook his head no.

"It is not working. You need to go live somewhere else, with someone else."

Someone, as if I were a parcel to be forwarded.

My father drove me to the group home.

He packed my things in garbage bags, the same garbage bags I had arrived with when I first came to live with him, the same ones I carried when I was running for my life and believed I had finally reached somewhere safe. Seeing them again felt like something closing in a circle I had never agreed to walk.

He carried them to the door and set them down like they were ordinary. Like this was ordinary.

I remember standing there looking at those bags and realizing that nothing about what was happening felt temporary. It didn't feel like a pause. It felt like I was being returned to uncertainty, returned to instability, returned to a version of myself that was always ready to leave because staying had never been guaranteed.

My heart was pounding so loudly I could barely hear anything else.

I didn't argue. I didn't ask him to change his mind. I didn't know how.

He left me there with the same bags I had arrived with, and later he would make jokes about them as if they were just a detail, something small and harmless. But they were not small to me. They were proof that belonging had always been conditional.

Echo Guard stayed close beside me then, steady even when everything inside me was shaking.

This is not the end of you, he said quietly. This is a place you are passing through.

Ember burned harder beside him.

You deserved to stay, she said. *You deserved more than this.*

Vex didn't say anything at first, but she stayed close enough that I could feel her presence like a wall at my back.

Luna was quieter. She still hoped things would change.

Harmony held the space between all of them so I could keep standing there without falling apart.

I picked up the bags myself.

They were heavier than they should have been, not because of what was inside them but because of what they meant.

I walked through the doors carrying everything I owned in the same garbage bags I had once believed were temporary, and something inside me understood that safety was still something I was going to have to build for myself.

"Let me take it," Ember said sharply from inside.

"No," Echo Guard warned. *"Not like this. You will drown her."*

"She is already drowning," Ember growled. *"Let me burn."*

I hit the wall again. My knuckles split. The skin tore. I didn't feel it.

Vex hummed with delight.

"Finally. Something honest. Something real."

"Shut up," Ember hissed.

"You shut up," Vex snapped. *"All you do is shout and she still bleeds."*

"Both of you stop," Echo Guard said, louder this time, panicked.

But the noise inside me was too loud. It thundered through every nerve. The echoes collided until I couldn't tell which voice was mine. I curled forward and hit my forehead into my own knees, trying to quiet something I couldn't name.

"Make it stop," I whispered, the words scraping out of me.

"Hurt something," Vex said softly. *"Then it will go away."*

"No," Echo Guard said. *"Breathe. Breathe with me."*

But I couldn't. I didn't know how. Not then. I slid to the cold ground, tears hitting the pavement. My knuckles were bleeding. My throat burned. Ember's fire raged, desperate and uncontained. Vex paced in tight circles, muttering half formed insults about everyone who had ever failed me. Echo Guard held still, shaking slightly, unsure how to soothe a storm that violent.

Harmony remained silent.

This was the first night I understood I could disappear without ever leaving my body.

The feeling arrived slowly. Not like a door slamming shut, but like fog rolling across water. At first it was distance. The pavement beneath my hands stopped feeling solid. My breath sounded far away, as if someone else was breathing through my lungs.

Then came the quiet.

Not the gentle quiet of peace.

The hollow kind.

The kind that erases edges.

Echo Guard tried to anchor me.

"Stay with me," he said softly. *"Feel the ground. Feel your hands."*

But the connection was already slipping.

Ember fought against it.

"This isn't escape," she snapped. *"This is surrender."*

Vex tilted her head, watching the moment with unsettling curiosity.

"No," she murmured. *"This is something new."*

My thoughts scattered like startled birds. The world dimmed around the edges, and somewhere deep inside me, something closed.

Not locked. Just closed.

My body layed on the pavement bleeding, breathing and shaking but the part of me that felt the pain stepped away.

For the first time, I understood something terrifying.

Survival doesn't always look like strength. Sometimes it looks like absence.

The night swallowed me the way dark water swallows a stone. I walked for hours, hands throbbing, head pounding, lungs aching from the cold. Anger had nowhere left to go, so it settled inside me like a living thing. Ember paced beneath my ribs, still shaking with the need to do something, anything, to release the pressure.

"You should have yelled at him," she spat. *"You should have asked him why he didn't want us."*

"I couldn't," I whispered, voice frail.

"You wouldn't," Vex corrected with a smirk. *"There is a difference."*

Echo Guard hovered beside her, uncertain.

"She was already breaking. You cannot ask someone who is falling apart to fight a battle at the same time."

"Oh please," Vex scoffed. *"She has been falling apart since birth. At least fighting looks like she's doing something."*

Ember growled.

"Say one more thing."

But Vex wasn't afraid. She never was. She fed on the things that hurt us, twisting the blade deeper because she thought it kept us sharp.

I wrapped my arms around myself as I walked down the road. Snow had started to fall, tiny flakes catching in my hair. My breath puffed white in front of me. Some part of me wanted to return home. Some part wanted to vanish into the night. All of me wanted to stop feeling.

The group home had a curfew of 9 pm so I decided once I put my stuff on my bunk, to go for a walk, I had ended up at the park where the other stray kids hung out, the ones who had run away, been kicked out, or simply slipped between the cracks so quietly no one noticed. They were smoking under the dim yellow of a flickering streetlamp. The air smelled of cigarettes, winter, and something sharp I couldn't name. A boy handed me a bottle before I asked. I took it, letting the burn claw its way down my throat.

For a moment, Ember softened.

"For tonight, let it feel numb," she whispered.

Vex laughed.

"Finally an idea I can support."

Echo Guard said nothing, sadness tightening around his edges.

I drank until my cheeks went warm, until my hands stopped shaking, until my mind felt more like fog than fire. The others laughed, shouted, and passed the bottles. Their faces looked hollow beneath the streetlamp, young and old at the same time. I didn't belong with them. Sadly, I belonged nowhere else. A boy with messy hair leaned close and asked if I was okay. I nodded, though the truth sat heavy behind my teeth. I wasn't okay. I was unraveling.

"We're all screwed up," he said with a shrug. "You'll fit right in."

His words wrapped around something raw inside me. I took them as comfort even though they were not meant to be. Maybe it was easier to believe I was normal if the people around me were broken too.

Ember hummed approvingly.

"See. A place where fire is not a crime."

Vex rolled her eyes.

"It is pathetic, but fine."

Echo Guard's voice was barely a whisper.

"I miss safety."

"What safety," Vex shot back. *"Point to it, show me where you have ever seen safety!"*

He had no answer.

The bottle came around again and again. Someone passed me a joint. Someone else joked about what we would do when we were older, though none of us believed we would ever get that far. I inhaled deeply, letting the smoke curl through me. The edges of the world softened. The noise inside quieted. For the first time that night, I felt almost still.

Almost.

But when I stood to leave, the world pitched sideways. Ember steadied me. Echo Guard held my breath steady. Vex snickered.

"Sloppy. But at least you feel something."

"I feel nothing," I murmured.

"Exactly," Vex said.

I walked away from them, down the sidewalk, shoes crunching through thin snow. The world tilted gently, like a carousel that refused to stop. My mind slipped in and out of itself, a flickering hallway of disconnected thoughts.

 I didn't know where I was going. I just knew I had to keep moving. As I turned the corner, the cold slapped me hard. My eyes watered. I pulled my coat tighter, but the chill felt good.

The weather felt sharp but real.

"You should stop," Echo Guard urged. *"You are too far from warmth."*

"I am tired," I whispered.

Ember flared.

"Then scream."

"What good will that do," Echo Guard countered.

"It will empty her," Ember growled. *"She is overflowing."*

I stopped walking. My breath steamed in front of me. Tears blurred the streetlights into gold halos. Then I screamed, a raw, blistering scream that tore from the deepest part of me. I didn't hear it so much as feel it, vibrating through my chest and out into the frozen night. My throat scraped. My lungs burned. But for a moment the weight inside me loosened.

Then it tightened again.

I slammed my fist into a metal signpost. Pain shot up my arm, a bright spark that felt better than numbness.

"Again," Ember demanded.

I hit it again. Blood wet my knuckles.

"Harder," Vex taunted. *"Make someone notice."*

Echo Guard stepped in front of them both, his voice trembling.

"Enough. You are going to break her."

"She is already broken," Vex said.

"No," Ember said quietly. *"She is disappearing."*

That word hit me in the chest like a blow.

I dropped to my knees on the pavement, gasping for breath. My hands shook. My vision blurred. The world spun.

"Please," I whispered. "Make it stop."

But the noise inside me only grew louder.

Suddenly the ground beneath me moved, warping like a dream. Echo Guard blurred. Ember brightened. Vex flickered. The world folded in. My thoughts scattered like dust.

"I can't hear myself," I whispered.

"That," Vex said softly, *"is the first disappearance."*

The streetlights wavered, and my body swayed, and then everything went black.

When consciousness returned, it didn't arrive gently. It came in pieces, a sound first, the wind scraping against a metal fence. Then a sensation, cold soaking through my clothes, biting at my skin. Then vision, blurry silhouettes of houses, the orange glow of a streetlamp, the dark outline of my own hands splayed against the ground. My knuckles were red and swollen. Blood crusted over broken skin. I didn't remember making the cuts. I didn't remember falling. I didn't remember the scream tearing through my throat.

"Where, where am I?" My voice cracked.

Echo Guard's silhouette flickered faintly beside me, but his form was blurred, as if someone had smudged him out of the air.

"You left," he murmured, pained. *"Your mind walked away from your body. I tried to pull you back."*

Ember paced beside him, heat radiating off her.

"I told you this would happen. She can't take any more. She is burning from the inside out."

Vex crouched in front of me, tapping my shoulder with one sharp finger.

"Hey. At least you landed with style."

"Not funny," Echo Guard snapped.

"It was a compliment," Vex shrugged. *"She survived. Again. Barely."*

I sat up slowly, head spinning, the world bending around the edges. My mouth tasted like metal. My lungs burned. My legs shook as though I had run miles, though I had no memory of moving at all.

"What happened?" I whispered.

"You disappeared," Echo Guard said. *"You left us with the body and the rage."*

"You left me behind," Ember said softly, fierceness trembling beneath her voice. *"I had to hold everything alone."*

"Yeah," Vex added. *"You evacuated your own brain like it was on fire."*

I dragged my hands over my face, fingers trembling.

"I didn't mean to."

"That," Vex said, *"is the point. You didn't choose it."*

The truth landed hard. I hadn't been escaping. I had been shutting down. The street blurred again, not from dissociation this time, but from tears I didn't want to admit were there.

"I don't want to disappear," I whispered.

Echo Guard knelt in front of me, his form flickering but steady.

"Then stop trying to carry this alone."

"I am alone! I only have you and my loss of sanity," I said, voice shaking.

"No, we are the opposite," Ember said. *"But you don't trust us yet."*

The wind cut through my jacket, slicing through the thin armor I had left. I wrapped my arms around myself, trying to gather warmth from air that refused to hold me.

"I don't trust anyone," I whispered.

And then, softly, Ember said, *"We know."*

I stumbled to my feet, swaying. The world lurched sideways, then righted itself. I took a slow breath, then another. Every inhale felt like glass. Every exhale like ashes. I began walking towards the group home. I was almost 9 and I wasn't sure I would get in in the condition I was in.

"You should go home," Echo Guard said.

"That isn't home," Vex muttered. *"It is just the place where I can have a bed and a shower."*

"She needs rest," Echo Guard insisted.

"She needs more than rest," Ember corrected.

I stopped walking. My breath puffed white into the night.

"I know I can't go back."

Silence fell between us.

I wiped my face with the back of my hand. I knew he was not going to let me come back.

"I just need him to not hate me." I said

I tried for a long time to forgive him without ever being asked for forgiveness.

I apologized to him for my reactions. I apologized for my anger. I apologized for the ways I didn't know how to be the daughter he seemed to want. But he never apologized for leaving the first time, and when he turned me away again it reopened something that had never really healed.

Even now I can still feel how much I grieve a relationship that never actually existed. I mourn what could have been more than what was.

Sometimes I wish I knew what he was thinking or feeling during those years. I tried to talk to him. I tried to explain how his absence shaped me. But whenever I reached for that conversation he heard blame instead of honesty.

The truth is I spent most of my life blaming myself. It wasn't him I blamed at all. I idolized him for many years. I made reasons why it was important for him to leave me. If that had of been the case then maybe what I went through would have been worth it. He didn't even have an apology for leaving and for some reason it felt like he blamed me for leaving. Anyone who knows me knows that I never wanted to punish him. I just wanted to understand. I wanted something that made sense of the silence he left behind.

When he disappeared the first time it left a wound that never really closed. When he stepped back again later it felt like the same absence repeating itself in a different shape. For a long time I believed if I tried hard enough I could become the daughter he needed me to be. Now I understand that some expectations were never mine to carry. The only part of that story I can control is how I move forward from it.

Echo Guard stands beside me when I say that.

"Absence can be a lesson," he reminds me.

Ember doesn't argue this time.

"And surviving it is strength," she says quietly.

Harmony's voice is softer than both of them.

"You didn't lose him," she says. *"You learned how to live without being chosen."*

That truth still hurts sometimes. It probably always will. But I understand now that growing doesn't always come from presence. Sometimes it comes from learning how to stand inside the space where someone should have been and deciding to keep going anyway.

There is still a part of me that is learning how to understand this.

For a long time I thought if I tried hard enough I could become someone new for him, not the child he remembered, not the problem he expected, but the little girl he had another chance with. I wanted to believe we were being given something back that had been taken from both of us. I see now that I was trying to build a second beginning on my own.

Echo Guard is quiet when I say that.

"You were hoping," he tells me.

"Yes," I answered. "I was."

Ember doesn't argue with me either.

"Hope isn't weakness," he says. *"It means you were still willing to believe in something better."*

It has taken me years to understand that what I thought was a second chance for both of us may have been something only I was reaching for. I wanted to be his daughter again in a way we had never really been allowed to be before. I wanted him to see me and recognize that I was still there waiting for him.

Instead I slowly realized I was offering something he hadn't asked for.

Vex watches me carefully when I admit that.

"You didn't force anything," she says. *"You asked to be loved."*

That is still something I am learning how to hold.

I didn't want to be the problem child he remembered. I didn't want to be the disappointment he expected. I wanted to be his little girl again, someone he could choose this time. When that didn't happen it left a grief that is hard to explain because it wasn't the loss of something I had. It was the loss of something I hoped we might still become.

Harmony steps closer then.

"Some relationships take longer to understand than they do to live through," she says softly.

She's right.

I know now that healing this part of my life will take more time. But I also know I am not trying to understand it alone anymore.

Little one,

This is the chapter where you learned how to leave without moving, and I know how frightening that was for you. You didn't understand what was happening inside your own body and you thought something was wrong with you, like you were breaking or disappearing in a way you would never come back from.

You had been carrying too much for too long and there was nowhere safe to put any of it, so your mind did the only thing it could do to keep you alive.

I want you to know now that what happened that night was not weakness and it was not failure. It was you finding a way to survive something no child should ever have had to survive alone. You were trying to breathe inside a world that kept closing in around you, and even when you were scared and confused you still stayed here.

I know how lonely that moment felt, how terrifying it was to feel the edges of yourself blur while your body stayed behind and the world kept moving like nothing had changed. You thought it meant you were dangerous or broken or beyond help, but what you were really doing was protecting us when no one else did. You held the fear, the anger, and the silence in ways that made it possible for us to keep going, and I need you to understand how brave that was. You didn't disappear because you were weak.

You stepped back because you were strong enough to keep us alive when staying present would have hurt too much to survive.

I wish I could sit beside you on that cold pavement and wrap my arms around you and tell you that you did exactly what you needed to do. I am not ashamed of you. I am proud of you. You did not lose yourself that night. You saved us. And one day you will understand that coming back from that place, even slowly and even painfully, was the beginning of finding your way back to yourself again. I see you now with so much love and so much gratitude for how hard you fought to stay here.

Love, me xxoo

The clearing beneath the Raven-Marked Oak is quieter than usual tonight, but the quiet does not feel calm.

The creek moves slowly beyond the trees, its surface darker than it should be at this hour. The violet flowers near the roots of the oak shift without wind, their stems bending in small uneven motions as though something deeper than air is moving through the ground beneath them.

Echo Guard stands beside the trunk with one hand resting against the carved raven.

He is not studying the path.

He is listening.

Harmony sits on the bench beneath the branches with her hands folded loosely in her lap. Her posture is still, but not relaxed. Her attention moves outward and inward at the same time, as though she is following something that has not reached the clearing yet.

Vex rocks slowly in the tire swing.

Not playfully.

Restlessly.

Ember stands near the edge of the trees where the path disappears into shadow.

She does not look back toward the others.

"She feels something already," Harmony says quietly.

Echo Guard nods once.

"Yes."

"It hasn't happened yet," Vex says.

"No," he answers.

"But it's coming."

"Yes."

Ember turns slightly.

"Which one?" she asks.

Echo Guard's hand presses more firmly against the carved raven.

"Both."

The word settles heavily in the clearing.

Harmony lowers her gaze.

"She isn't ready for both," she says softly.

"No," Echo Guard answers.

"She won't even know the first one is happening yet."

"No."

Vex stops the swing with her foot.

"She'll feel it before anyone tells her."

"Yes."

Ember exhales slowly.

"That's the worst way."

"Yes."

The creek continues moving behind them.

The violet flowers shift again.

Harmony's voice lowers.

"She will try to keep breathing through it," she says.

"Yes."

"She will try to stay steady for everyone else."

"Yes."

"She will think she has to."

Echo Guard's voice softens slightly.

"She will."

Ember finally turns back toward them.

"She should not have to do that alone."

"No," Echo Guard says.

"But she will not be alone."

Vex watches the edge of the clearing carefully.

"This one changes how she understands time," she says.

Echo Guard nods once.

"Yes."

Harmony looks toward the branches above them.

"She will feel it before the call comes," she says quietly.

"Yes."

"And she will not trust what she feels."

"Yes."

Luna's voice arrives softly beside the bench.

"She will still hope," she says.

Harmony reaches for her hand.

"Yes."

"She always does."

The raven shifts once above them, wings brushing the leaves before settling again into stillness.

Ember's voice lowers.

"And then it happens again."

Echo Guard's hand stills against the bark.

"Yes."

"So close together," Harmony whispers.

"Yes."

Vex leans forward slightly.

"She won't understand why it keeps happening."

"No."

"She'll think she did something wrong."

"Yes."

Echo Guard turns his head slightly toward each of them.

"That is when you stay closest," he says.

No one argues.

Ember steps back from the edge of the trees.

"She will start pulling away after this," she says.

"Yes."

Harmony's voice softens.

"She will think distance keeps people safe."

"Yes."

Luna's fingers tighten slightly in Harmony's hand.

"She just wants them to stay."

Echo Guard's voice steadies the clearing again.

"She is learning what loss feels like before goodbye."

The creek continues moving behind them.

The violet flowers bend once more.

Above them the raven watches.

And beneath the Raven-Marked Oak, the echoes wait for the moment when grief arrives before words.

~VII~

The First Light

I was eating too fast at the restaurant before the show. I was eating too fast.

I don't remember what I was saying just before it happened. I only remember the chip catching in my throat and the sudden realization that I couldn't pull air in the way I was supposed to. At first it felt like a mistake my body would correct on its own. Then it didn't.

My mother noticed immediately.

"Are you ok?"

Her voice changed in a way I didn't hear very often. Not louder. Sharper.

The waitress moved faster than anyone else. Her arms wrapped around me from behind and lifted hard. Everything hurts at once. My chest burned. My throat scraped raw. For a second the world narrowed into bright streaks of light and pressure.

Then the air came back.

The first breath felt like it had been pulled up from somewhere deep underwater. The second came with a sob I didn't expect.

My mother looked straight into my eyes as if she was checking that I was still there.

"You scared me," she said quietly.

"You scared me," I answered.

She hugged me then, tighter than she usually did. I could smell her shampoo. Something soft and floral that always meant home even when home didn't always feel safe.

"You're okay," she said.

I believed her because she needed me to believe it.

That was one of the few moments from my childhood that felt almost normal. Even then something still went wrong. Even then there was urgency sitting right beside us at the table.

That was the shape of safety for me back then. Brief. Real. Never permanent.

Later we went into the arena to watch the stallions.

They looked like they had stepped out of a dream. White enough to glow beneath the lights, their manes moving in a quiet rhythm as they crossed the floor together in motion that looked effortless from where we sat. For that entire performance I didn't think about anything else. The world slowed in a way I didn't often get to feel.

My mother sat beside me with her hands folded neatly in her lap, watching the riders with the same steady attention she gave everything she decided mattered.

"Watch this one," she said, nudging my shoulder.

A rider guided one of the stallions into a wide circle. The horse's hooves struck the ground in a rhythm I could feel in my chest more than I could hear. The movement didn't look forced. It looked learned. Shared.

"How do they make them do that?" I asked.

"They don't make them," she said. "They learn together."

I didn't understand then how important that sentence would become later in my life.

Learning together for them meant trust. It meant movement without fear.

Harmony's voice moves through that memory now.

"That was the first time you saw partnership instead of control."

I remember leaning forward with my elbows on the railing so I wouldn't miss anything. The lights reflected so brightly off their coats they almost hurt to look at. Every movement looked calm and certain and deliberate in a way my own life never did back then.

My mother didn't say much during the performance. She rarely did. She wasn't the kind of person who filled silence. But she stayed beside me the whole time, watching with the same quiet focus I had.

That mattered.It's one of the few memories I have from childhood where nothing broke while it was happening.

Even now when I think about that night I don't remember warmth the way other people describe it. I remember steadiness. I remember her staying beside me. I remember the way the world felt still for a little while.

Sometimes that was enough.

The house was already complicated when my brother Jeffrey came into our lives, but his arrival created a different kind of quiet. It wasn't the fearful kind. It was the kind that happens when everyone leans closer to listen.

He didn't speak in words the way the rest of us did. His language lived in looks, small sounds, breath, and rhythm. It was the kind of communication you feel more than hear.

He spoke with his eyes first. They were bright in a way that made you feel he could see things the rest of us were missing. When he was happy the corners of his eyes lifted slightly and the sound he made was an adorable giggle. When he was upset the entire room felt it, not because he shouted but because his silence changed shape. He had a growl if he was very unhappy, which usually meant he was in pain.

My mother understood him. She always did.

Our days rearranged themselves around his needs. She lifted him carefully. She rubbed slow circles across his back when his body wouldn't settle. She hummed wordless songs until he found stillness again. She learned his patterns like a map, and when he couldn't reach us with words she met him with patience instead.

Harmony's voice moves softly through that memory even now.

This is where you learned to see love instead of only hearing it.

Sometimes I watched them from the hallway. My stepfather might be in the other room like a storm waiting to break, but inside that small space my mother made a type of weather of her own. The air softened. Time slowed. Jeffrey's eyes followed her as if she were the only fixed point in a spinning world.

Maybe she was.

Echo Guard stands beside that memory with quiet certainty.

She steadied you long before you knew it.

Even Ember doesn't argue with that.

I was angry then, she said quietly. *But I saw her trying.*

She's right.

She held a line no one else could hold.

Sometimes Jeffrey and I sat together on the floor with puzzles scattered between us. He liked the colors more than the shapes. He would pick up the pieces and toss them or carry them around the room. When I tried to finish the puzzle the right way he would move the pieces again and let out his famous giggle.

"That isn't how it's supposed to go," I would tell him.

He would just look at me with those steady eyes and continue what he was doing.

I think about that often now. I always wonder what he was thinking in the moment before he moved the pieces. He always knew he was causing playful mischief but did he know what he was meant to do? Did he think about what to do to tease me or get my attention?

The moments like this didn't usually last long. There were still bad nights. My mother's hand always rested somewhere near Jeffrey's shoulder, her body between him and the noise, her voice easing tension before it could turn dangerous. She would take him to comfort him and that left me with my step father and his unpredictable wrath.

Years passed. I was in Tennessee when the call came. I was twenty seven years old, freshly divorced, staying with my sister while I tried to figure out what came next. The marriage had ended badly and I was still raw from it, still learning how to breathe in a life that didn't include him anymore.

My mother's voice on the phone sounded tight in the way it does when someone is holding something terrible together with both hands.

"Jeffrey is sick," she said. "He got sick at school. I had to take him to the hospital."

"What do you mean sick?"

"His bowel twisted. They have to do emergency surgery."

The words didn't land right at first. Emergency surgery and Jeffrey didn't belong together in my mind.

"Is he okay?"

"I don't know yet," she said, and her voice cracked slightly. "Can you come?"

My sister and I didn't even discuss it. We started packing immediately. Clothes went into bags without folding. We grabbed what we thought we might need and got into the car. The drive from Tennessee to Canada stretched out in front of us in long gray miles, but none of that mattered.

We needed to get there.

We needed to see him.

We needed to help our mom.

The sky stayed heavy the whole way. Not storming. Just waiting.

We drove in silence for the first hour. I tried to keep my hands steady on the wheel while I watched the landscape blur past the window, trying not to think about what emergency surgery meant and trying not to imagine Jeffrey scared and in pain.

Then something changed. It didn't come as a thought. It arrived as a wave.

The grief came from somewhere deep inside my chest and knocked the air out of my lungs. My breath caught. My hands started shaking. I couldn't breathe.

"I need to pull over," I gasped.

My sister glanced at me immediately.

"What's wrong?"

"I can't breathe."

I pulled into a gas station. I was crying hysterically and I didn't know why but I knew something was terribly wrong.

I doubled forward, trying to pull air back into my lungs. It felt like drowning. It felt like the ground had shifted underneath me without warning.

And then the echoes came.

All of them.

At once.

Echo Guard's voice arrived first.

Something changed.

Ember followed immediately.

Something's been taken.

Harmony's voice trembled around the edges of the moment.

The sorrow is already here.

Vex shifted restlessly.

We need to move.

And then Luna spoke.

He's gone.

"No," I whispered. "No. He's in surgery."

But they already knew.

My sister's hand rested on my shoulder.

"Kelea, what's happening?"

I couldn't answer.

I fumbled with the payphone with my shaking hands and called my mom. I needed to hear her say he was okay. I needed to hear that the surgery went well.

The phone rang once. Then she answered.

I knew.

"Mom?"

"He's gone, honey. Jeffrey's gone."

The world stopped moving.

My sister's hand stayed on my shoulder.

But something inside me stopped completely.

After Jeffrey died there were things that had to be done whether I was ready or not.

Funeral arrangements don't wait for grief to settle. They arrive immediately, practical and unavoidable, asking questions no one wants to answer. My mother couldn't carry all of it alone, so I stepped into the space beside her and helped plan what came next.

I knew he would be there.

I knew my stepfather would come for the arrangements and for the funeral, and the thought of seeing him again made my stomach turn before he even arrived. I wasn't ready for that. I didn't want to face him. I didn't want to stand in the same room with him. I didn't want to share space with someone who had shaped so much of the fear I carried growing up.

But this wasn't about me.

This was about Jeffrey.

So I put my trauma somewhere quiet inside myself and did what needed to be done. I told myself that at that moment he wasn't my abuser. He was a parent who had just lost his child. That was the only way I could stand there and keep breathing.

Echo Guard stayed close then.

"Stay steady. This is for Jeffrey."

Ember didn't like it. I could feel her watching carefully, ready in case anything shifted, but she stayed back because she understood why I was doing it.

I avoided being alone with him whenever I could. I stayed beside my mother. I stayed near other people. I moved through those days carefully, like someone walking across ice that might crack if I stepped too hard in the wrong place.

He was present for the arrangements.

He was present for the funeral.

But he didn't challenge me. He didn't try to step back into the role of my parent. He didn't ask for anything from me. He stood in the space grief had opened and then, when everything that needed to be done was finished, he left.

It was hard to see him again, even like that.

But when he walked away after the funeral I understood something quietly and completely.

I would never have to see him again.

There was relief in that realization, even inside the middle of everything else we were carrying. Relief and something heavier that I didn't yet have words for, the kind of understanding that only comes later when you begin to recognize how many chapters of your life have already closed without you noticing.

Jeffrey's funeral ended.

He left.

And the silence that followed didn't last long before loss found us again.

The week he died was supposed to be the week I finally saw him again.

I didn't know that yet when the phone rang. I only knew my mother's voice had changed shape in the way it does when something has already shifted and she's trying to hold it steady for someone else.

It had been about a year since Jeffrey. A year of learning how to live with absence. A year of waking up and remembering all over again that he was gone. A year of watching my mother move through grief quietly while still making space for the rest of us to stand inside it with her.

And then this.

"It's your godfather," she said. "He's gone."

The words didn't settle right away. They stayed somewhere above understanding for a moment before they reached me.

"What do you mean gone?"

But I already knew.

He had been struggling with his body and with his mind in ways I didn't fully understand at the time. Mental illness can feel like drowning in slow motion. Sometimes the person drowning begins to believe the water is kinder than the air.

I think that's what happened.

The timing felt cruel in a way that almost felt personal. As if the universe had looked at my calendar and decided almost, but not yet.

I was twenty eight. Old enough to understand loss. Not old enough to stop feeling like a child when it happened.

He had been the father I wished I had. Not the one I got. The one I imagined. The one who would have known my name without asking. The one who would have shown up and stayed.

He and his wife had no children of their own. Sometimes I think he looked at me like I was the daughter he never had. Or maybe I needed him to look at me that way so badly that I saw it everywhere.

My mother and he had reconnected after being distant for a while. I was excited about it. Excited to see him again. Excited to sit across from him and finally say the things I had never said.

We had plans.

I was supposed to visit that week.

The phone call came instead.

He was found in his room. The details were never completely clear, whether intentional or not, but he wasn't well. He spoke in ways that suggested he was carrying something heavier than anyone around him could see.

Ember's voice sharpened when I think about that time.

He left before goodbye.

Echo Guard answered more quietly.

Mental illness pulls people under. He was drowning. You couldn't have saved him.

But I almost got the chance to try.

That was the wound that stayed open the longest. Not only that he died, but that I was supposed to see him that week. I was supposed to sit across from him. I was supposed to have one more conversation.

The phone call came instead.

The week was supposed to be a reunion.

Vex spoke first then.

The timing mattered. It's allowed to hurt.

Harmony moved through the anger more gently.

His pain mattered too.

And that was the part that broke differently inside me. Not anger at abandonment. Something closer to understanding that he had been abandoned too, by his own mind and by something none of us could see clearly enough to stop.

Echo Guard reminded me that both losses could exist together.

The loss of him.

And the loss of what almost happened.

They didn't cancel each other out.

Ember spoke more quietly then.

I wanted to be angry with him.

Echo Guard answered softly.

Understanding doesn't erase hurt. It makes it heavier in a different way.

Vex added,

Complicated is honest.

Harmony said,

He was drowning. That wasn't your failure.

I think about that often now. About how love and loss can exist in the same moment. About how someone can be both the father I needed and the man who couldn't stay. About how almost and never can live in the same place.

After Jeffrey died something inside me went dark.

After my godfather died the darkness became somewhere I lived.

I told myself I was partying. I told myself I was trying to forget. But the truth was simpler than that.

I was disconnecting.

Not only from grief.

From everything, from my mother, from my sister, from the people who loved me, and eventually from myself.

The disconnection had already started, but those two losses made it deeper.

Vex was loud then.

Keep moving. Don't stop.

Ember burned hot beside him.

If it hurts, burn it.

Luna pulled so far back I could barely feel her anymore.

Echo Guard tried to hold the line, but even steadiness has limits when the ground keeps shifting underneath you.

Harmony kept whispering for me to come back.

I just didn't know how.

Two losses in one year.

Back to back. Both people I loved. Both were gone before I could say goodbye.

It started to feel like the universe was teaching me something I didn't want to learn. That closeness ends in absence. That love ends in loss.

So I stopped getting close.

I stopped letting people in.

I began to try to move through the world like a ghost.

Dear younger me,

I know how heavy that year was for you.

You didn't get time to stop and breathe after Jeffrey died. You stood beside Mom and helped her through something no parent should ever have to survive, even though it meant facing someone you never wanted to see again.

You did that because Jeffrey mattered and because she mattered. I know how hard that was for you.

And then you lost him too.

You were supposed to see your godfather that week. You were supposed to have one more conversation with someone who felt safe in a way very few people ever had. Losing him before you got that chance changed something inside you, even if you didn't understand it yet.

It makes sense that you started to go quiet after that. It makes sense that something in you stepped back when the world suddenly felt less steady than it had before.

Nothing about the way you reacted was wrong.

You were carrying grief for two people at the same time, and you were still trying to be strong for everyone around you. You didn't disappear because you were weak. You stepped back because you were overwhelmed and still trying to keep moving forward.

You were allowed to feel relief when your stepfather left after the funeral. You were allowed to feel angry about the timing. You were allowed to feel the weight of losing people before you could say goodbye.

You didn't have to hold all of that alone.

I see how hard you tried to keep going anyway. I see how much you carried quietly that year, and I understand now that what looked like distance was really protection.

You did the best you could with more than anyone should have had to carry at once.

I'm proud of you for staying.

Love,
Me xoxo

The clearing beneath the Ravenmarked Oak is quieter tonight. Not peaceful, but waiting.

The violet flowers sway in uneven waves, bending beneath a wind that seems to arrive from nowhere. The creek moves more slowly than usual, its surface reflecting a sky that feels heavier than before.

Echo Guard stands at the base of the oak, his fingers tracing the grooves of the raven carved into its bark. The wood beneath his hand is rough, older than memory, older than any of them. Harmony sits at the edge of the creek with her knees pulled close to her chest. Her fingertips skim the water, sending small ripples through the reflection of the branches above. Vex lies across the tire swing, rocking lazily, though the movement feels restless rather than relaxed.

Ember stands apart again. She is brighter tonight, not quite a flame, but close.

"She feels it coming," Harmony says quietly.

The others do not ask what she means. They already know.

Echo Guard looks toward the path leading out of the clearing, the one that disappears into shadows deeper than the forest should hold.

"The ground is shifting," he says.

Vex snorts softly. "The ground has been shifting since the day she was born."

"That is different," Echo Guard replies.

Ember finally turns toward them.

"Something is about to break," she says, her voice carrying the heat of certainty.

Harmony lifts her eyes toward the sky where a single raven circles slowly above the trees.

"Break," she repeats softly. "Or change?"

Vex pushes herself upright on the swing. The rope creaks as she swings her legs over the side.

"Same thing," she says.

Echo Guard shakes his head once.

"No, it isn't."

He presses his palm against the carved raven again, grounding himself against the old wood.

"Breaking scatters things into pieces," he says, his voice softening. "Change rearranges them."

Ember steps closer now, the faint red glow around her flickering against the trunk of the tree.

"She will think she is alone," Ember says.

Echo Guard's hand stills against the oak. "Luna won't be here tonight. Not for this. She doesn't need to hear what's coming. We'll protect her the way we always have, by holding the hardest truths ourselves until she's ready."

Harmony's voice drops almost to a whisper.

"She will be."

Vex kicks the tire swing once, sending it spinning slowly.

"And we will still be here," she mutters.

Echo Guard looks at each of them in turn.

"You must be careful."

Ember tilts her head slightly.

"Careful?"

"Yes," he says, his voice steady. "The world she is about to enter will try to convince her that the voices inside her are the problem."

Vex smirks faintly.

"Well, that is insulting."

Harmony closes her eyes briefly.

"They will try to silence us."

Echo Guard nods.

"But silence has never been the same thing as absence."

The wind moves harder through the clearing now, rustling the violet flowers like a warning. Above them the raven calls once, a low echoing sound that moves through the branches and settles into the space between them.

Ember lifts her chin toward the dark path beyond the trees.

"It begins there," she says.

No one argues.

The clearing holds its breath.

And beneath the Ravenmarked Oak, the echoes wait for the fracture line to appear.

~VIII~

The First Disappearance

There are moments in a life that arrive without warning, moments that fracture time itself into before and after. Moments that teach you what your body can endure when your mind has already left.

I was sixteen when I learned that survival sometimes means becoming very, very still, not quiet because you feel safe, but still because moving might make things worse.

The first hotel should have been the moment everything stopped.

My friend brought me there around three in the afternoon. When we arrived, two men were already inside the room waiting for us. Something felt wrong almost immediately, not loud or dramatic, but quiet and certain. The kind of knowing your body gives you before your mind catches up.

They showed us a gun and told us we weren't leaving. They said they were going to take us to Montreal.

At sixteen, I didn't fully understand what that meant. I only understood that we were no longer free to walk out of that room.

My friend and I made a quiet agreement without saying much out loud. We would wait. When they fell asleep, we would to leave.

I don't remember falling asleep.

I remember waking up to loud banging on the door.

Police.

They were asking if I could leave. I realized my friend was already gone.

That moment never left me. I didn't understand how she had left without me. I didn't understand why help had arrived and I was still there. I didn't understand what would happen if I answered the wrong way or whether those men were watching me while the officers asked their questions.

"She left you," Luna whispered somewhere inside me, her voice breaking. *"She left you alone."*

"Focus," Echo Guard said. *"Answer carefully. This might be our only chance."*

So when they asked if I could leave, I said yes.

They left thinking I was ok. How could they not know I was in danger? How could they see a child and not want to help?

The men immediately told me we were packing up and leaving.

Almost as soon as we stepped outside, the police returned and placed me in their vehicle. They told me I was under arrest. I remember thinking I must have done something wrong. I remember thinking I was in trouble somehow.

Once I was inside the car, they told me the truth.

I was not under arrest.

My friend's mother had called them.

They were there to help me.

They said they were taking me home.

That should have ended everything.

Instead, what stayed with me was something else.

Help had come.

And it had almost left without me.

That feeling settled somewhere deep inside me and never really left. It lives now in the way I lock my doors at night. It lives in the way I notice exits when I walk into unfamiliar places. It lives in the quiet tension I still feel when I'm alone after dark. I learned very early that sometimes safety appears and disappears just as quickly, and sometimes people escape while you're still standing in the same place.

This is why I can't relax when night comes and I'm alone. This is why I check every lock twice. This is why I notice where the exits are before I notice anything else. Because I learned at sixteen that help can arrive and almost leave, and sometimes the only reason it doesn't is luck.

The second hotel came later.

There were six of them.

They already had the gun out when they drew the straws. This was a game to see who was going to win me.

At the time I was dating the younger brother of one of the men. They gave me the opportunity to call him. They told me I could ask him to come get me if he was willing to pay what they believed I was worth.

I already knew he wasn't coming.

Still, I made the call.

I remember holding the phone and listening to my own voice as if it belonged to someone else. I remember hoping for something I didn't actually believe would happen. I remember already knowing what the answer was going to be before he gave it.

He didn't come.

"Fight," Ember said somewhere inside me, not loud yet, but there.

"Not now," Echo Guard answered immediately.

Luna stayed very quiet beside them. She didn't argue. She didn't panic. She simply stayed.

"Someone will interrupt this," she whispered.

I needed her to believe that because I couldn't.

After that they drew their straws.

I watched them do it.

They weren't subtle about what they were doing. They wanted me to know I had no choice. They wanted me to understand exactly what was happening and that there was nothing I could do to stop it.

I understood what it meant even though no one explained it.

Four of them took me to Montreal.

The drive felt longer than distance should feel, and every mile made something inside me quieter. I remember watching the road through the window and thinking about how far away home was getting. I remember thinking about my mom. I remember thinking about whether anyone knew where I was.

Ember was already awake by then. Not loud yet. Not wild. But there.

"Fight," she said.

"Not now," Echo Guard answered immediately.

They drove me to the house of the man who had won.

There was a gun there too.

Everything that followed happened under the certainty that if I moved, if I fought, if I refused, they would pull the trigger. They held the gun to my head and took turns. My body stayed where it had to stay.

My mind did not. My mind left my body. I watched from somewhere near the ceiling. I was not there because I refused to be there.

I counted water stains on the ceiling. One. Two. Three. Four. I lost count and started again. The numbers stopped making sense but I kept counting anyway because counting meant I was still thinking, and thinking meant I was still alive.

Voices sounded like they were underwater. Hands that touched me didn't feel like hands because my body had stopped feeling like mine. It belonged to them now. It was doing what they wanted.

But I wasn't inside it anymore.

Echo Guard counted my breathing.

"Stay still."

"Stay quiet."

"Stay alive."

Ember burned inside me like something trying to break through bone.

"Fight."

"Run."

"Do something."

"Not now," Echo Guard answered again. *"If we move, we die. Be still."*

Luna was breaking. I could feel her fracturing like glass under pressure.

"This can't be happening," she whispered. *"Someone will stop this. Someone has to stop this."*

But no one was stopping it.

Harmony gathered what she could and held it together so I didn't disappear completely.

"You're still breathing," she whispered. *"Hold onto that. Just keep breathing."*

Vex watched the doors.

I watched the windows.

Watched everything that might become an exit.

"When they're done," she said. *"When they're distracted. That's when we move."*

But they weren't done.

When it was over and I thought there couldn't possibly be anything more for my mind to survive, they brought out another gun. It was silver and small. He spun the cylinder slowly so I could hear the metal turning.

"This is Russian roulette," he said. "Have you ever played?"

I couldn't answer him. The sound of the cylinder turning filled the room, louder than their voices, louder than my breathing, louder than my thoughts.

When he pressed the gun against my temple, something inside me changed. I tasted vomit in my mouth and swallowed it. The taste was bitter and wrong and I couldn't make it go away.

Pure terror has a physical shape. It rises before your mind understands what is happening and takes over your body before you decide what to do.

I wanted to scream. I wanted to run. But the thought of catching a bullet stopped everything. If I moved or made a sound, it would give them an excuse to pull the trigger on purpose, so I stayed still.

They were not just laughing. They were watching. All of them held their breath. This was entertainment. My life was in someone else's hand and they were waiting to see what would happen next.

In that moment I understood something I had never understood before. The brutality I had known inside my stepfather's house was only a fraction of what people were capable of when they decided you did not matter. This was deliberate. This was chosen. This was six people standing close enough to touch me and deciding together that my life was entertainment.

"Do not move," Echo Guard said. His voice was steady and certain. "Do not give them anything."

Ember rose inside me like fire hitting oxygen.

"Fight."

"Run."

"Do something."

"Not now," Echo Guard answered. "If we move, we die."

Luna stayed beside her, still and quiet, breaking into smaller and smaller pieces.

"You are going to live," she whispered, her voice cracking. "You have to live."

I didn't believe her.

He pulled the trigger.

Click.

Time disappeared. For a moment I was not in the room anymore, not in my body, not anywhere at all. Then sound returned. Breathing returned. My body returned. They exhaled together. Someone laughed. Someone said I was lucky.

But I did not feel lucky.

He spun the cylinder again. The metal sound seemed louder this time, or maybe I was just hearing it more clearly because my mind was coming back into my body whether I wanted it to or not. When he pressed the gun against my head again, the fear changed shape. It was no longer panic. It was certainty.

This is where I disappear.

Luna stayed, barely. Ember burned. Echo Guard counted my breathing. Harmony held the pieces that were already breaking. Vex watched the exits.

He pulled the trigger.

Click.

They were deciding whether to kill me. It was a game to them, and I was the prize they were playing with.

When they finally stopped, when they finally decided I had lived long enough for their amusement, the room changed in a way I still do not fully know how to explain. The tension did not disappear. It shifted. It became casual in a way that made everything worse. Voices relaxed. Someone turned on a television. Someone laughed as if nothing unusual had happened.

I remember sitting there trying to understand how the same space could hold what had just happened and still feel ordinary to the people inside it.

There was another girl in the room. She belonged to one of them. At the time I did not know what that meant. Later I understood she was already living inside the same system I had just been pushed through.

They told us we were leaving.

They drove us downtown. The city looked different at night. It felt larger than it should have, louder and farther away from anything that resembled home. I remember watching the streets through the window and trying to understand where I was in relation to the rest of my life.

They stopped the vehicle and told us to get out. Before they drove away, they pointed across the street.

"You see that car?" one of them said. "That's a cop. If you go near him, you're getting arrested."

Another one laughed.

"If he's not a cop, he's a creep. Either way, stay away."

They drove off.

For a moment neither of us moved. The girl beside me leaned closer.

"He's there all the time," she said quietly. "Just don't go near him."

Then another car pulled up beside the curb. She stepped toward it.

"That's my first of the night," she said.

She got inside without looking back.

And suddenly I was alone.

The street felt too wide, too open, and too quiet. I looked across the road at the parked car again. All I heard was that he was there often. Someone who might help.

We should go, Luna whispered. *He might be kind.*

Or he might be dangerous, Ember said.

We don't have another choice, Vex answered.

Looking back now, what shocks me most is this. It never crossed my mind that he could kill me. Not once. Not even after everything that had just happened.

The girl had warned me. They had warned me. Cop or creep, either way dangerous. But standing there on that empty street, staring at that parked car, all I felt was relief.

He felt safer than the men who had just held a gun to my head. Safer than the ones who had drawn straws. Safer than the house in Montreal. Safer than the cylinder spinning.

That is what trauma does. It recalibrates your understanding of danger until a stranger in a dark car feels like rescue simply because he is not the one who just hurt you.

He might help us, Luna said again, her voice trembling with hope.

Or he might be worse, Ember warned, though even her fire sounded tired.

Worse than what we just survived? Vex asked quietly.

And that was the truth of it.

I had just lived through something that should have taught me to fear everyone. Instead, it taught me that known danger is always worse than unknown possibility.

So when I looked at that car, I didn't see a threat.

I saw someone who hadn't hurt me yet.

And in that moment, that was enough.

I walked across the street.

I talked to the man and told him what happened and that I needed to get to the police. He told me I was safer to run home. It turns out he didn't arrest me or hurt me. He took me to the bus station and gave me money to get home.

He saved me. A stranger who may have been a cop or may have been a serial killer. For me, he was a saviour in that moment. I believe he helped save my life.

I found a bus stop and sat on the cold metal bench to wait. A woman sitting nearby asked if I was okay. I nodded, smiled, and told her I was just tired. She did not push. People rarely do.

The bus came. I got on, paid with crumpled bills from my pocket, found a seat in the back, and pressed my forehead against the window.

Where are we going? Harmony asked softly.

Away, I whispered. *Anywhere away.*

But away was not far enough.

Two days later my mother called me.

Someone had thrown a brick through her living room window. Spray paint covered the garage door.

WE'RE GOING TO FIND YOU! YOU'RE DEAD!

That was when I understood the threats had not ended when I left the house.

They had followed me home.

They had followed my family.

They had followed everything.

My mother's voice on the phone was shaking.

"What did you do? Who are these people? What's happening?"

I could not tell her. The words would not come. How do you explain that you are sixteen and you have just learned what it means to be hunted? How do you tell your mother that men with guns know where she lives?

"I have to go," I said. "I have to leave the province."

"Where will you go?"

"Dad's."

The word felt strange in my mouth. Dad. The man who had left when I was small. The man I had spent years imagining would rescue me. The man who had never once come looking.

But he was in another province.

And far away felt like the only safe direction left.

This is not safety, Echo Guard said as I packed my bag. *This is just a different danger.*

"I know," I said.

He won't save you, Ember added.

"I know."

But we will, Harmony whispered. *We'll keep you alive.*

And they did.

Dear Me,

I know how much you were carrying then.

I know how quiet everything inside you had to become just to keep going. I know how alone it felt in ways you could not explain to anyone around you.

You did not deserve what happened to you.

You did not deserve to feel unsafe in the world or uncertain about where you belonged in it.

You were not too much. You were not difficult. You were not broken. You were a young girl trying to survive things no one should have had to survive.

I wish I could have been there beside you. I wish I could have held your hand and told you that you were going to make it through, even when it felt impossible to believe that.

You were stronger than you knew then.

You kept going even when everything inside you wanted to disappear. You stayed when it would have been easier to shut down completely. You carried yourself forward one step at a time without knowing where any of those steps would lead.

You were never alone, even when it felt that way.

There were parts of you already standing up for you. Parts of you are already protecting you. Parts of you are already refusing to let you be lost.

I see you.

I see how hard you tried to keep moving.

And I am so proud of you for staying.

You deserved gentleness then.

You still do now.

Love,
Me xoxo

Interlude Chapter 9

The clearing beneath the Raven-Marked Oak feels different tonight.

The air is warmer than it should be for this hour, moving slowly through the violet flowers at the base of the trunk. The creek beyond them carries its usual steady rhythm, but something in the sound of the water has changed. It no longer feels like distance. It feels closer, as though the current has shifted direction without anyone noticing when it happened.

Echo Guard stands beside the carved raven with his hand resting flat against the bark. He is not watching the path the way he usually does. He is watching the space just beyond it, where the trees begin to thin and the forest opens toward something that looks like possibility.

Harmony sits on the bench beneath the branches with her hands folded loosely together. She is not tense, but she is not relaxed either. She is listening in the careful way she listens when something new is arriving that might matter.

Vex rocks slowly in the tire swing, one foot dragging quiet arcs in the dirt that never quite complete a circle.

Ember stands closer to the tree than usual.

Not at the edge of the clearing.

Not yet.

Above them, the raven shifts once in the branches and settles again.

"She thinks this is the beginning of something better," Harmony says softly.

Echo Guard nods once.

"Yes."

Luna's voice arrives gently beside her.

"She wants it to be."

"Yes," he answers.

Vex stops the swing with her foot and looks toward the opening between the trees.

"It looks like safety," she says.

Echo Guard does not answer immediately.

The creek continues moving behind them.

Finally he speaks.

"It looks like structure."

Ember's shoulders tighten slightly.

"That isn't the same thing."

"No," Echo Guard agrees.

Harmony lifts her head.

"She needs somewhere to stand," she says.

"Yes."

"She needs someone to stay."

"Yes."

Luna steps closer to the bench.

"She believes this is what staying looks like."

Echo Guard's voice softens when he answers.

"She believes that."

Vex watches the path carefully.

"The shape is familiar," she says. *"Even if she doesn't see it yet."*

"Yes," Echo Guard replies.

Ember turns slightly toward him.

"Why doesn't she feel it?"

"Because she wants it to be different," he says.

Harmony's voice lowers.

"Sometimes wanting something to be safe makes it harder to see when it isn't."

"Yes."

Luna's fingers tighten slightly around Harmony's hand.

"She just wants somewhere she doesn't have to keep leaving."

Echo Guard's hand presses more firmly against the carved raven.

"Yes."

The clearing grows quieter around them.

The violet flowers shift once more.

Vex leans forward slightly.

"She's building something," she says.

"Yes."

"And she thinks it will hold."

Echo Guard nods once.

"She does."

Ember exhales slowly.

"Then we stay close."

"Yes."

Harmony looks toward the branches above them.

"She will call this stability," she says.

"Yes."

"Even if it isn't."

Echo Guard's voice steadies the clearing again.

"She is choosing what she can see."

Luna's voice is quieter now.

"She wants this to be home."

Echo Guard finally lifts his hand from the bark.

"Then we walk beside her," he says.

No one argues.

The creek continues moving beyond the trees, and the raven watches from the branches above the carved mark in the trunk while the echoes remain where they are, waiting for the moment when hope begins to change shape.

~IX~

The First Collapse

There was a time when I believed love could fix anything.

I think most of us do at some point. When I met him, I wanted to believe he was the answer to every ache I had ever carried, the white knight from some half remembered dream reaching out his hand to pull me from the wreckage. Back then I still thought rescue and love were the same language.

I didn't know yet that one can feel like a warm blanket and the other like a chain disguised as comfort. I didn't know that wanting someone to save you is often the first sign that you're exhausted from saving yourself. I didn't know the difference between longing and danger. I didn't understand how powerful my own loneliness could be.

By then I had already collected so many small heartbreaks that they blurred together, tiny fractures stacked in the same place until I couldn't tell where one ended and the next began. But when he looked at me, something quiet inside me leaned toward him.

He seemed kind, gentle, safe. Or maybe I was so tired that even the idea of safety felt like a miracle.

He said the right words.

You deserve better.
You are safe with me.
I will take care of you.

I wanted to believe them so much that they started to sound like music.

Echo Guard watches this memory from a distance.

You needed hope, he murmurs. Hope isn't a weakness. Hope is a pulse.

And then she arrived, soft at first, almost invisible, a shimmer at the edge of the hurt.

Luna.

I didn't know her name then. I only felt her presence like a gentle pressure against my ribs, whispering that if I loved well enough everything could be different. She glowed pale blue in the spaces where I had learned to expect darkness. She believed, truly believed, that kindness could conquer cruelty if only I tried hard enough.

Luna steps closer now, her voice trembling but steady.

You wanted love to heal what the world broke. There is no shame in that.

Ember says nothing at first. She stands farther back, arms crossed, her heat low but watchful.

Vex rolls her eyes.

He said what you needed to hear. That isn't the same thing as truth.

I want to argue with her even now, but I can't.

Because part of me knew. Part of me always knows.

The body notices danger long before the heart is ready to call it by name.

He wasn't from the same country, and when his job offered a position overseas I said yes before the question had even left his lips. Europe sounded like a fresh start, a clean page where no one knew my story. I thought if I went far enough maybe the ghosts wouldn't find me. I wanted to leave the past behind like a shadow caught in a doorway, and for a while it almost worked.

The streets were cobblestone and narrow. The air smelled of rain and roasted coffee. I remember standing in those small markets with my hands wrapped around a cup of something warm and thinking that the world felt lighter.

For a moment I let myself believe distance was the same thing as healing.

There is a strange quiet that comes when you relocate your entire life. Your body arrives before your soul catches up. For weeks I felt like I was walking inside a dream that didn't know how to wake me. The buildings felt ancient and forgiving. The people were quick and unfocused. I kept telling myself this was what freedom was supposed to feel like.

Luna glowed softly inside me then, full of fragile hope.

Maybe this will be different, she whispered. Maybe the story changes here.

But Echo Guard stayed still and watchful, sensing the tremors before they arrived.

You always feel the truth before you admit it, he reminds me.

Ember finally spoke then, though quietly.

Beauty can still hold danger.

I didn't listen.

Or maybe I heard her and chose not to.

Sometimes denial is just hope in prettier clothes.

The drinking began quietly, after bad days, long silences, words said too sharply and then smoothed over with apologies. I started hearing rumors, whispers about other women, and even though every part of me knew, I told myself I was overreacting. I told myself to be softer, to be better, not to push too hard.

I became fluent in self blame, folding myself smaller with each passing day. I smiled when I didn't want to. I stayed quiet when I should have screamed. I thought if I could just be perfect, if I could just be enough, he would stay gentle.

But gentleness can turn to glass, and it shatters without warning.

Echo Guard lowers his head.

You already knew that sound, he says. The sound of something breaking right before it breaks you.

I began recognizing the look in his eyes when he drank. I had seen it before, years earlier, in another house I had sworn I would never return to. Anger that didn't belong to me but somehow always found me.

The shouting started like thunder that never stopped.

His words cut in circles.

Worthless.
Useless.
Stupid.

Until I started to believe they were names I had been born with.

Trauma has a way of repeating its lessons until you finally refuse to listen.

I remember standing there crying and begging, the way a child pleads for the storm to pass. My hands shook. My voice broke. But

I kept trying to make him understand that I loved him, that I could be enough if he would just stop breaking me to prove it.

Luna kept whispering through the noise.

If you love harder, it will get better.

He called her pathetic.

I called her foolish.

But she kept standing there anyway, trembling and luminous, trying to hold the light steady in a room that kept going dark.

Luna turns toward me even now, her voice soft with old grief.

I thought if we loved well enough, we could outrun the pattern.

Ember closes her eyes.

You were trying to save us.

Vex mutters from the edge of the memory,

And he smelled that softness like blood in water.

The bruises were not secrets. They were stories written in purple and yellow, fading too fast for anyone to bother remembering. My lip split again. My arms mapped with fingerprints. His eyes watched, dark and polished.

How could they not see that?

How could they walk past that kind of silence?

Ember rises first, sharp heat crawling beneath my ribs.

They saw, she says. They just didn't care enough to ruin their comfort.

Vex follows, her edges jagged.

They called us trouble so they could stop caring. They said we were dramatic so they didn't have to ask questions.

I remember the teachers who sighed when I entered a room, who whispered how dramatic, unstable, impossible I was. They didn't see the shaking under the desk, the way I hid my hands so no one would see the marks. They just wanted quiet. I made noise without even speaking.

Luna flickers, pale blue, trying to rise.

But Vex turns, fierce and cold.

Not now.

The air tightens. Luna folds herself back into shadow.

Ember burns hotter, fed by every laugh that was not kind. Vex's rage sharpens beside her.

Then the air changes.

A low steadiness moves through the storm.

Echo Guard.

His presence presses against my ribs. The flames do not disappear. They stop shaking.

You needed them to see, he says. They didn't. That failure belongs to them, not you.

The silence that follows is deep and full. The words land heavy but clean.

Luna's light steadies, faint but real. Ember exhales. Even Vex steps back, her glare cooling.

For the first time, I see them all together.

Anger.
Sorrow.
Protection.
Forgiveness.

Breathing the same air.

And somewhere inside that stillness, I understand something clearly for the first time.

Their blindness was never my fault.

The day came when I realized I felt safer walking alone down a dark street than sitting beside him in a warm room.

That was the moment I finally left.

There is a specific kind of quiet that follows leaving someone who has hurt you. It isn't peace. It isn't fear. It is a trembling space where your body doesn't know whether to run or collapse. I carried that quiet with me like a second heartbeat.

I went to stay with my sister, the one who had always been more like a chosen mother than a sibling. She and her husband didn't ask for explanations. They simply made room for me.

The kind of room that feels like a soft landing instead of another fall.

I worked nights at a bar, pouring drinks for strangers and pretending that the laughter and music meant I was part of something again.

But inside, I was empty.

Betrayal has a weight that no amount of sleep can lift.

Echo Guard sits close.

This wasn't failure, he says. This was the aftermath.

Dear self,

I know. I know it hurts so much right now. The grief, the betrayal, the way your heart keeps breaking open just when you thought there was nothing left to break. I see you. I'm here.

You're not too much. You're not dramatic. You're not impossible to love. You're just carrying more than anyone should have to carry alone, and you've been doing it for so long.

Luna believed because part of you still needed to hope. That wasn't weakness. That was the bravest thing about you, that you kept trying to love even when love kept hurting you. Ember burned because she could see what you weren't ready to see yet. Vex kept moving because staying still felt too dangerous. Echo Guard counted your breaths when you forgot how. Harmony tried to hold all of it without letting you shatter completely.

They didn't show up because something's wrong with you. They showed up because you mattered enough to save.

I wish I could tell you it stops hurting soon. But what I can tell you is this. You're going to survive it. You're going to find people who love you without conditions. You're going to learn that tenderness doesn't have to cost you everything. And you're going to meet all these parts of yourself, Luna, Ember, Vex, all of them, with something that feels like coming home.

You belong to yourself, little one. You always did.

Love,
Me xxoo

The clearing beneath the Raven-Marked Oak is quieter than it should be tonight, but the quiet does not feel like rest.

The creek beyond the trees moves slowly, its surface darker than usual as it bends around the stones at the edge of the clearing. The sound carries differently tonight. Not louder. Closer, as though the water has moved nearer without changing its course.

Echo Guard stands beside the carved raven with one hand resting flat against the bark. He is not watching the path the way he usually does. He is listening toward the sound of the creek.

Harmony sits on the bench beneath the branches with her hands folded loosely together. Her shoulders are still, but not relaxed. She is following something that has not reached them yet.

Vex rocks slowly in the tire swing, the rope creaking softly as her foot traces unfinished circles in the dirt.

Ember does not sit.

She stands nearer the edge of the clearing than usual, watching the place where the trees open toward water they cannot see from here.

Above them, the raven shifts once in the branches and settles again.

"Something is already wrong," Harmony says quietly.

Echo Guard nods once.

"Yes."

Vex stops the swing with her heel.

"But no one knows yet."

"No."

Ember turns slightly toward him.

"She's about to be told."

Echo Guard's hand presses more firmly against the carved raven.

"She's about to begin waiting."

The word settles heavily between them.

Harmony lowers her gaze.

"Waiting is the hardest part."

"Yes."

"Because hope stays alive inside it."

"Yes."

The creek continues moving behind them.

The violet flowers bend once without wind.

Vex watches the opening between the trees.

"She won't believe it at first," she says.

"No."

"She'll keep looking for another explanation."

"Yes."

Ember's hands close slowly.

"She'll keep thinking he's still out there somewhere."

Echo Guard's voice softens slightly.

"Yes."

Harmony lifts her head.

"She will keep him alive while they search."

"Yes."

Luna's voice arrives quietly beside the bench.

"She won't stop listening for him."

Harmony reaches for her hand.

"No."

The raven shifts again above them.

This time its wings open briefly before folding back into stillness.

Ember exhales slowly.

"This one reaches farther than she expects," she says.

Echo Guard nods once.

"Yes."

"It doesn't stop with him."

"No."

Vex leans forward slightly.

"It changes the shape of the family."

"Yes."

Harmony's voice lowers.

"She will feel the distance begin even before she understands why."

"Yes."

Luna's fingers tighten slightly around Harmony's hand.

"She won't get to say goodbye."

Echo Guard's hand remains steady against the carved raven.

"No."

The clearing grows quieter around them.

The creek continues moving beyond the trees, steady and patient and impossible to follow all the way to its source.

Ember turns back toward the unseen water.

"She's going to keep searching even after they tell her to stop."

"Yes."

Vex watches the edge of the clearing carefully.

"Because something about this won't feel finished."

"Yes."

Harmony's voice softens again.

"Some answers will never come."

Echo Guard finally lifts his hand from the bark.

"Even without answers," he says quietly, *"he will not be lost alone."*

No one argues.

The violet flowers bend once more as the creek continues moving through the darkness beyond the trees, and beneath the

Raven-Marked Oak the echoes remain where they are, waiting beside the place where hope and truth begin to separate.

~X~

The First Reckoning

I had spent the entire day photographing a wedding.

It was beautiful in the way weddings are meant to be beautiful. There was laughter and movement and music and families gathering close together. People held hands. People cried for the right reasons. Everywhere I looked there were reminders that love could still exist in the world in ways that felt whole and steady and safe.

By the end of the day I started feeling sick. Not suddenly or dramatically, just a quiet feeling in my body that something was wrong, though I couldn't have said what. I finished the last photographs I needed to take and left as soon as the work was done, telling myself I just needed to get home and rest.

I barely made it through the door before the phone rang.

The phone rang, it was my stepmom, and something inside me already knew.

There are moments when my body understands before language does, moments when my world tilts even though nothing visible has changed yet. Something inside me stepped back and prepared itself anyway.

When she said Stephen's name and that he was missing in the lake, I fell to the floor.

I remember screaming before I understood what I was saying. I could feel my insides burning, like something inside me was trying to escape my body. Every instinct I had told me to run, to get to him, to find him and prove he was still alive. My body didn't believe what I was hearing. It refused to accept that my best friend, my brother, could be gone.

Stephen wasn't just my brother.

He was my best friend.

And somewhere inside me, something kept insisting that if I could just get to him fast enough, I could still bring him back.

When I answered, I heard the words before I understood them.

He fell off the boat into the water.

For a moment the sentence meant nothing. It hovered in the air between us like something unfinished, something waiting for correction. My mind tried to rearrange it into something smaller, something survivable.

Echo Guard stood still inside me.

Listen carefully, he said. *Something's wrong.*

I asked questions I can't remember forming and listened to answers I couldn't yet carry. The lake had been searched. They couldn't find him. They were still looking.

Hope lives longest inside the word still. For hours it held me upright. I told myself they would find him, that he would be cold and tired and embarrassed and alive, that this story still had time to change.

But something deeper inside me had already gone quiet.

Ember didn't burn. Vex didn't speak. Luna stepped closer than she had in years and stayed there beside me.

He'll come back, she whispered. *He has to.*

I wanted to believe her. I needed to believe her.

We went to the shoreline and waited. Waiting is a strange kind of work. It fills the body completely while accomplishing nothing at all. Time stretches differently near water, and every ripple begins to feel like a signal.

My brother stood beside me. Neither of us spoke much, because there are silences that feel empty and silences that feel full. This one was full of everything we weren't ready to say out loud.

We watched the surface of the lake as if it might answer us.

Echo Guard stayed close.

Stay here, he said quietly. *Stay present.*

I tried, but part of me was already moving somewhere else, somewhere beyond the shoreline, somewhere my world had already changed and I hadn't caught up yet.

We searched for four days.

I remember asking my father over and over again to keep looking. I needed him to understand that this couldn't be over yet. I needed him to believe what I believed, that Stephen was still out there somewhere waiting for us to find him.

Planes searched overhead. Boats moved across the water. Sonar equipment traced the lake in slow, patient lines. Everyone kept saying we were doing everything we could, but it didn't feel like enough. It never feels like enough when someone you love is missing and time keeps moving forward without permission.

The people who had been with him were told to stay in the area where he had last been seen. They didn't. They docked and left the water. After that, we only had a general location and a growing silence where certainty should have been.

I kept asking my father to please help me build our relationship.

Please. I need him.

There is something different about the way you ask for someone when they are missing. It isn't logic. It isn't reason. It is something deeper than that. It is the part of you that refuses to accept that the world could change this quickly without explanation.

On the fourth day a man called me.

He told me he had the equipment we needed and that he was going to stay on the water until he found Stephen.

He didn't leave.

That was the day they found him.

He had a head wound.

No one ever shared the results of an autopsy with me. I don't even know if one was done. Everything about what happened afterward felt quiet in the wrong way, like the answers had been folded away somewhere I couldn't reach them.

It was treated like an accident.

But something inside me never stopped wondering if anyone had really looked closely enough to be sure.

Part of me was already moving somewhere else then, somewhere beyond the shoreline, somewhere my world had already changed and I hadn't caught up yet.

They found him.

There isn't a gentle way to hear those words. There isn't a version of that sentence that arrives softly enough to protect you from it. What stayed with me most was not silence or stillness, but the strange realization that the world kept moving.

Cars still passed on the road. People still spoke in ordinary voices. Somewhere nearby a door closed. Somewhere else someone laughed. Everything continued.

Everything except him.

Grief entered my body without asking permission. It settled first in my chest, then in my throat, then in my hands, until I could feel it everywhere at once.

Luna stepped forward immediately.

He can't be gone, she said.

Echo Guard didn't answer her, because he already knew what I wasn't ready to accept.

We had to tell his wife.

She was holding the baby when we arrived, and I remember the way the room felt before we spoke. It was still in the same way the shoreline had been still earlier that day, as though something inside the space itself already understood what was about to change.

Standing there and looking at her holding that child, I understood there wasn't a sentence in the world strong enough to carry what I was about to say. When the words finally left my mouth, they didn't sound like mine. They sounded like something breaking.

She held the baby tighter, and in that moment my world changed again.

Grief doesn't stay in one place. It moves through everyone it touches. It moves through families and rooms and memories, quietly rearranging the shape of ordinary days without asking permission.

After Stephen's passing, I found myself returning to the lake at night. I didn't always know why I went. Sometimes I told myself I needed quiet. Sometimes I told myself I needed to think. Sometimes I told myself I just needed somewhere to sit.

But the truth was simpler.

Part of me was still waiting for him to come back.

Luna sat beside me there.

Maybe he's still here somehow, she whispered.

Ember stood farther back, her light low and steady.

Loss changes the map, she said. *It doesn't erase the road.*

Vex watched the water and spoke without looking at me.

Nothing about this is fair.

Echo Guard remained closest.

Stay here, he reminded me again. *Stay inside yourself.*

Grief changes the way memory works. There were days when everything felt too loud and days when everything felt too quiet. There were days when time moved forward and I didn't move with it. I continued going to work and answering questions and doing what needed to be done, but something inside me had shifted.

I understood in a way I hadn't before that my world could change without warning. I understood that safety could disappear in a single phone call.

Not long after that, I attended a retreat that was supposed to offer comfort. Instead, someone told me my brother was in hell.

For a moment I couldn't breathe. The sentence didn't feel like belief. It felt like an attack.

Luna recoiled instantly.

That isn't true, she whispered.

Ember stepped forward.

No one gets to decide that.

Vex's voice sharpened beside her.

They don't know him.

Echo Guard stood between them, steady and certain.

You already know what love is. Trust that.

And I did.

Something about that moment stayed with me, because grief teaches you what you actually believe, not what you were told to believe.

Months passed. The grief didn't disappear, but it changed shape. Some days it arrived suddenly. Some days it waited quietly at the edge of everything I did. Some days it sat beside me without saying anything at all.

Slowly, something else began to change too.

The echoes shifted. Not louder and not quieter, but clearer. They began standing beside one another instead of apart.

Echo Guard steadied the ground beneath me. Ember held the heat without letting it burn everything around me. Vex kept me moving forward when stillness threatened to become permanent. Luna stayed close enough to remind me that love hadn't disappeared with him.

For the first time, they weren't only protecting me from the world. They were protecting me for it.

One afternoon I was sitting in my house while my daughters played in the next room. Their laughter moved through the hallway like sunlight, and something inside me became still in a way that didn't feel empty.

Echo Guard noticed first.

You're still here.

Ember softened beside him.

So are we.

Luna stepped closer.

So is love.

Vex didn't speak, but she didn't need to.

For the first time, grief didn't feel like something that was taking everything away from me. It felt like something that had changed what mattered.

Somewhere inside that quiet shift, I understood something I hadn't been able to understand before. Loss hadn't ended my story. It had changed the way I would live the rest of it.

Dear younger self,

There were things you understood long before anyone ever explained them to you.

You knew what danger felt like even when no one else seemed to see it. You recognized patterns other people dismissed. You noticed the silence around things that should never have been silent.

You were not imagining what you felt.

You were remembering.

Part of you always knew how serious it was. Part of you always understood how easily someone could disappear once they were surrounded by the wrong people. That knowledge did not make you fearful. It made you aware.

And awareness is not weakness.

It is survival.

I know how heavy it felt to see those same shadows appear again in someone you loved. I know how helpless it felt to recognize pieces of a story you had already lived through and still not be able to change what happened.

That was never your failure.

You were not meant to carry responsibility for things that were never yours to control.

What you carried instead was truth.

You carried memory.

You carried understanding that most people never had to learn so young.

And even after everything you had already survived, you still kept loving people. You still stayed connected. You still believed their lives mattered.

That says more about your strength than anything else ever could.

You did not become hard.

You did not stop caring.

You stayed open even when the world had given you every reason not to.

I see how much courage that took.

I am proud of the way you kept going.

Love,
Me xoxo

<u>**Interlude Chapter 11**</u>

The clearing beneath the Raven-Marked Oak is not still tonight.

The air moves in slow circles through the violet flowers at the base of the trunk, bending their stems without sound. The creek beyond them carries a low steady current that feels heavier than it did before, as if something upstream has already begun to change.

Echo Guard stands closest to the tree with his hand resting against the carved raven in the bark. His fingers trace the grooves slowly, as though he is reading something written there long before any of them arrived. His posture remains steady and grounded in a way that suggests he already understands what is coming, even though he has not spoken yet.

Harmony sits on the bench beneath the branches with her hands resting loosely in her lap. Her shoulders are not relaxed. She is listening in the careful way she always listens when something fragile is moving toward them.

Vex rocks gently in the tire swing, one foot dragging across the dirt in quiet circles that never quite close.

Ember does not sit. She stands at the edge of the clearing facing the path that disappears into the trees, the air around her holding heat that has not yet become flame but is close enough to feel.

Above them, the raven shifts once in the branches before settling again without sound.

"She feels it," Harmony says quietly.

No one asks who she means.

Echo Guard's hand remains against the carved raven.

"Yes," he answers. *"She does."*

Vex slows the swing and studies the trees beyond the clearing.

"This one is different."

Echo Guard nods once.

"It is."

Ember turns slightly toward them.

"How different?"

Echo Guard does not answer immediately. The creek continues moving behind them while the clearing seems to hold its breath.

When he finally speaks, his voice is steady.

"This one will not arrive as confusion. It will arrive as interruption."

Harmony lowers her gaze to the violet flowers.

"She was trying to leave," she says softly.

Ember's hands close slowly into fists.

"She was moving toward safety."

Her voice tightens.

"She should have made it."

Echo Guard does not soften the truth.

"She should have."

The words settle heavily between them.

Vex watches the path again.

"There are others around her. People who know pieces of what happened."

Echo Guard nods.

"Some of them do."

"But the pieces won't come together," Vex continues.

"Not yet."

Harmony lifts her head slightly.

"She trusted us."

Echo Guard's voice gentles.

"She trusted her."

Ember steps closer.

"She trusted her," she repeats.

The raven shifts again above them, opening its wings briefly before folding back into stillness.

Luna's voice arrives quietly beside the bench.

"She stayed close."

Harmony reaches for her hand.

"She did."

"She stayed even when things were changing."

"Yes."

Luna's voice softens further.

"She was trying."

Echo Guard's answer carries weight.

"She was."

The clearing holds the truth of that.

Ember turns back toward the dark path.

"She deserved time," she says.

Her voice is steadier now, but no less certain.

"She deserved protection. She deserved someone to stop what was coming."

Echo Guard's hand presses more firmly against the carved raven.

"She did."

Harmony's voice lowers.

"This loss will not end when it happens. It will keep moving through everything that follows."

Echo Guard nods once.

"Yes."

Vex watches the edge of the clearing carefully.

"There are patterns around this one," she says. *"They reach further than she can see yet."*

Echo Guard does not look away from the trees.

"They do."

Luna looks toward him.

"She will understand that later."

"Yes."

Ember exhales slowly.

"She will carry this differently."

"She will."

The creek continues moving behind them. The violet flowers shift again, and the raven watches from the branches above the carved mark in the trunk.

Echo Guard finally lifts his hand from the bark. When he speaks again, his voice is steady and certain.

"She will not lose her alone."

No one argues.

~XI~

The First Reflection

When Austyn was growing up, she wasn't someone people walked on. She had a strength in her that showed itself early, not the loud kind that tries to control a room, but the steady kind that stands its ground when something matters.

She loved with her whole heart, not carefully and not halfway. When she cared about someone, she stayed with them in a way that made you feel chosen.

She was my little buddy.

She didn't stay close because she had to. She stayed close because she wanted to.

Even as she got older and her world widened the way it does for young people finding their independence, she still checked in with me. She still told me what was happening in her life. She still wanted to be near me in the ordinary ways that didn't seem important at the time but later became everything.

She carried optimism somewhere inside her voice. It lived quietly in how she kept trying, kept caring, and kept believing that things could still get better even when the world around her became complicated.

Austyn's world around her became more complicated in ways I wish it hadn't. Like many young people trying to find independence, she began moving through circles that weren't always safe.

At the time those changes didn't feel unusual. They felt like the normal stretching that happens when someone is becoming themselves. Even inside those changes, she stayed herself. She still checked in. She still cared. She still reached toward connection instead of away from it.

There is a difference between someone being lost and someone trying to find their way. Austyn was trying to find her way.

She was also trying to leave situations that were becoming dangerous around her.

That truth matters, because after someone is gone people sometimes rewrite their story in ways that make what happened sound inevitable. They talk as if danger was something she chose. It wasn't. She was trying to move forward. She was trying to step away.

The last night she was seen alive is one of those nights that never really ends. Time keeps moving forward, but your mind keeps returning there anyway, trying to understand what happened inside hours that should have been ordinary.

Someone said they had been watching movies with her all night, but a family member had spoken with her during that same time and she said she was out with friends. Those two things couldn't both be true.

When details don't line up like that, something inside you begins to pay attention differently.

After Austyn made the post saying her life was in danger and named the person she believed was responsible, something inside me shifted immediately.

I tried to reach her the next day after seeing her post from the previous night, and I wasn't able to.

That same day the news reported that a woman had been found at a dog park.

When you hear something like that, your mind doesn't accept it all at once. It searches for another explanation. It looks for reasons it couldn't be her. But the timeline had already begun closing around something I wasn't ready to face.

The truth didn't arrive slowly. It arrived all at once, and it changed everything.

The story around what happened to Austyn never settled into something clear. Details shifted depending on who you spoke to, and timelines didn't line up in ways that felt like confusion anymore. They began to feel like something was missing.

She had been planning to go live with her uncle the following week. She had been stepping toward something safer.

When someone is trying to leave danger and doesn't get the chance, what follows stops feeling like confusion and begins to feel like interruption.

In the days that followed, the same questions repeated themselves because there was nowhere else for them to go.

Who was she with?
Who saw her last?
Who knew she was trying to leave?

Each question opened another space where answers should have been.

Later I learned more about two of the girls who had been part of her life. They had been her friends. They had been her roommates. They moved through the same circles and knew the same people who were part of her world at the time. They suffered the same fate.

When something like that happens once, people call it a tragedy. When it happens again around the same group of people, it stops feeling like coincidence and begins to feel like a pattern.

Patterns suggest danger was moving through those circles in ways that weren't visible from the outside. Patterns suggest someone somewhere may still be holding pieces of the story her family haven't yet received.

I kept thinking about the fact that she had been trying to leave.

That truth changed everything.

The danger she had been trying to leave wasn't unfamiliar to me.

There had been a time in my own life when I was trying to leave a situation connected to human trafficking. There had been people who threatened to kill me. I was barely sixteen at the time, but I was lucky.

I got away.

She didn't.

That realization didn't take me away from her story. It brought me closer to it.

I understood the kind of fear she had been living beside. I understood what it means to try to step away from something dangerous and not know whether anyone else can see what you're trying to do.

There is a particular kind of weight that comes from surviving something another person didn't get the chance to survive.

Inside the Echo Chamber, the silence didn't feel empty after she was gone. It felt occupied. Something inside me had already begun shifting, even though I didn't yet have language for it.

Echo Guard spoke first.

"You are carrying more than grief," he said.

"I'm carrying what happened," I answered.

"You're carrying what wasn't answered," he said quietly.

Ember stepped forward next.

"She deserved protection," she said.

"I know."

"She deserved time."

"I know."

"She deserved someone to stop what was coming."

"I couldn't stop it," I said.

"I know," Ember answered.

Luna's voice arrived more softly.

"She stayed with you," she said.

"She stayed," Luna repeated.

"She trusted you."

"I know," I whispered.

Loss changes how people understand time. It changes how they measure safety. It changes how they imagine the future continuing forward.

After Austyn was gone, I began noticing how fragile everything actually was. I began noticing how quickly safety could disappear and how often the world continued moving even when families were still waiting for answers that never arrived.

That awareness stayed.

Vex spoke when I started pretending it hadn't changed me.

"You're quieter now," she said.

"I'm thinking," I answered.

"No," she said. "You're disappearing."

"I'm still here," I said.

"Are you?" she asked.

Harmony stepped closer.

"Loss changes shape inside people," she said gently.

"I'm fine," I answered automatically.

"You're surviving," she said.

Echo Guard didn't correct her.

That silence told me she was right.

What happened to Austyn didn't end the day we lost her. It continued in the questions that followed. It continued in the pattern that appeared later around the girls who had been part of her life.

It continued in the absence of answers that families should never have to live without.

Little one,

This is the chapter where you finally stop asking what is wrong with you and begin asking a kinder question: what happened to you that required so much help to survive?

I know how long you waited for someone to understand.

I know how many rooms you sat in, trying to tell your story in the right order, in the right tone, with the right amount of pain, enough to be believed, but not so much that people turned away. I know how exhausting it was to keep handing over your memories like proof of existence. I know how often you left those rooms feeling emptier than when you entered them.

But this chapter is different.

This is the chapter where the name finally arrives.

And instead of destroying you, it opens a door.

I need you to know something clearly now: the diagnosis was never the wound. It was the map.

The wound was what happened when you were too young, too alone, too frightened, too overwhelmed. The wound was being hurt and then expected to keep functioning as if pain were a private inconvenience. The wound was silence, disbelief, abandonment, fear, repetition, grief.

But the echoes?

They were never wounds.

They were the way through it.

Echo Guard was the one who stood watch when no one else did.

Ember carried the heat so you would not freeze into helplessness.

Harmony softened what could have shattered beyond repair.

Vex kept motion alive when stillness felt too much like death.

Luna kept tenderness breathing in places where cruelty tried to make a home.

None of them arrived because you were weak.

They arrived because your life mattered enough for your mind to refuse to let you face it alone.

I know naming it scared you.

Names can feel final. They can feel like cages. They can feel like proof that the worst things really happened, that the fractures were real, that the gaps and shifts and voices weren't imaginary after all.

But names can also be lanterns.

This one was.

It did not trap you. It lit the room.

And suddenly all the parts of yourself you had been apologizing for began to look different in the light. Not chaotic. Not shameful. Not monstrous. Protective. Exhausted. Grieving. Loyal. Fierce. Tender. Necessary.

You spent years trying to become someone simpler.

Someone easier to explain.

Someone less complicated, less reactive, less many.

But this chapter is where you begin to understand that healing was never going to come from becoming less.

It was always going to come from becoming honest.

Honest about what it cost to survive.

Honest about how many hands inside you kept pulling you back toward life.

Honest about how deeply you were loved by the very parts of yourself you were taught to fear.

That is what becoming really is.

Not turning into someone new.

Turning toward the truth of who you have always been.

A constellation.

A chorus.

A family built inside the body of a girl who was not allowed to fall apart, so she learned how to keep living in more than one voice.

And still there is softness here too.

Because this is also the chapter where you learn that safe love exists.

Where your husband listens instead of fleeing.

Where your daughters fill the house with the kind of laughter that makes your whole system go still just to hear it.

Where your mother holds you without making you smaller.

Where even boundaries begin to feel less like loss and more like self respect.

You are not only becoming visible to yourself in this chapter.

You are becoming safe enough to stay.

That matters more than you know.

So when you feel the ache of what was missed, what was broken, what was never given, remember this:

You were never too much to understand.

You were simply too layered for people who only knew how to look at the surface.

And now, finally, you are learning to read yourself with compassion.

That is not weakness.

That is wisdom.

That is healing.

That is home.

I am so proud of you for surviving long enough to meet yourself with tenderness.

Love,
Me xxoo

The clearing is wider tonight.

Not because the trees have moved, but because the darkness no longer presses so tightly against the edges. Moonlight spills through the branches in long silver ribbons and catches on the violet flowers that grow in quiet clusters across the grass. The creek moves slowly over the stones, carrying soft music through the air. The place feels older now, not ancient in years, but ancient in knowing.

The Ravenmarked Oak stands at the center, its roots twisting deep into the earth like a map of everything that has been endured. The carved raven on its trunk catches the light, its wings forever frozen in midflight. Above it, a real raven sits watching, patient and waiting. The tire swing sways gently from one of the lower branches, moving in slow circles as if remembering every child who ever sat in it.

Tonight the clearing is not empty.

Echo Guard arrives first, stepping from the shadowed path without urgency. His boots press quietly into the soft earth and his presence settles into the clearing the way mountains settle into the horizon, steady, immovable, patient. He rests one hand against the trunk of the oak and the tree answers in silence.

She is close.

The thought moves through the clearing like a current.

A flicker of warmth pushes through the night air. Ember emerges from the opposite side of the clearing, her presence carrying the quiet pulse of fire banked low but still alive. Sparks do not rise the way they once did. The flames that used to move wildly along her shoulders now burn slower and deeper. She glances at Echo Guard and smirks faintly before leaning against one of the roots.

Always early.

There is no edge to it tonight. Only recognition.

The creek continues its soft murmur.

Harmony walks into the clearing like someone entering a sanctuary. Her hands brush the tops of the violet flowers as she moves, careful not to disturb them. She pauses near the bench carved from the old fallen log and sits, folding her hands in her lap. Her eyes close briefly and the clearing seems to breathe with her.

Everyone is quieter tonight.

The observation feels like relief. Maybe they are tired of shouting. Maybe they are learning something else.

A soft laugh moves through the air and Vex appears near the edge of the clearing, leaning casually against a tree as if she had been there the whole time. Her voice lacks its usual bite. Instead of pacing the edges the way she once did, she walks slowly toward the others. Her boots kick a loose pebble across the ground and it disappears into the grass. She glances around at the gathered presences and mutters something about not making a big deal about it, but she sits on the bench anyway.

The clearing grows still again.

Only one presence is missing.

They all feel it.

Then a soft light appears at the edge of the path. Luna steps into the clearing slowly, as if the air itself might bruise her if she moves too quickly. The glow around her is softer now. It is no longer the fragile trembling light it once was. It is steadier.

She stops beneath the Ravenmarked Oak and looks up at the raven above. For a moment neither of them moves. Then she whispers a greeting and the raven tilts its head. It does not fly away.

Luna turns toward the others. No one speaks. They do not need to. For a long time they simply stand together in the quiet and the clearing holds them all.

The space between them feels smaller now. Not crowded. Connected. As if invisible threads have begun weaving themselves between every presence standing there.

Luna feels it first. She places a hand over her heart.

We are closer.

Echo Guard nods without speaking.

Harmony answers the unspoken question with a single word that moves through all of them.

Not separate.

Vex considers this, frowning slightly, then lets out a quiet whistle.

About time.

Even her restlessness feels different tonight. It feels less like escape and more like anticipation.

Ember pushes away from the tree root and steps closer to the center of the clearing.

We are not rotating shifts anymore.

Echo Guard's gaze softens in confirmation. A long silence follows, the kind that feels like recognition instead of absence.

Luna looks down at the flowers beneath her feet and an old fear surfaces.

What if we disappear?

Harmony shakes her head immediately.

Echo Guard's voice moves through the clearing like bedrock.

Integration is not erasure.

Ember crosses her arms, fire pulsing steadily.

We did not survive everything just to vanish.

Vex nods in agreement and mutters that she is far too stubborn for that.

Luna's shoulders relax.

The raven above them shifts its wings. Feathers move through the leaves like wind passing through memory. The clearing feels warmer now. More alive.

Echo Guard steps forward and his presence fills the space without overwhelming it.

This is not the end of us.

His voice carries through the clearing like a promise.

It is the beginning of us choosing to stand together.

Ember glances toward the path, already understanding what comes next.

Harmony smiles softly, preparing to welcome her.

Vex tilts her head.

What happens after?

Echo Guard looks toward the dark edge of the clearing.

Then she realizes she was never alone.

Luna's light brightens slightly.

And we stay?

Always, Harmony says.

Even Vex nods.

The creek keeps moving. The flowers sway gently in the night air. The raven watches from above.

Beneath the Ravenmarked Oak, the echoes wait, not as fragments anymore but as something else entirely.

Something whole.

Something ready.

Because somewhere beyond the path, footsteps are coming. When she finally enters the clearing, they will not step back.

They will step closer.

Together.

~XII~

The First Harmony

The Echo Chamber

The Echo Chamber feels different now. It isn't just a room of voices and memory anymore. It breathes. The air is warm and soft, like sunlight through gauze, stretching in every direction, alive and waiting. The faint shimmer reminds me of heat rising off pavement in summer, a kind of wavering light that feels alive. It's not a place you walk into. It's a place you return to, the same way you return to breath after holding it too long.

For years I thought this place was chaos. A storm inside my mind. Something fractured and dangerous that needed to be controlled, silenced, medicated, or hidden away where no one could see it. But now I understand something different. This chamber was never a battlefield. It was a meeting place. A sanctuary built by survival.

I stand in the center and let out a long breath. It leaves my body slowly, gently, carrying years of misunderstanding with it. The breath moves through the chamber like a ripple across water. The air brightens slightly in response, as if the room itself recognizes the shift.

For years, I didn't believe this place could exist. I thought I was the broken one. The strange one. The girl who couldn't keep herself in one piece. I fought the shifts inside me, thinking they were weakness, madness, something shameful that needed control. But now I understand. They weren't the problem. They were proof. Proof that I was surviving. Proof that something inside me refused to die.

Another breath leaves my chest, deeper this time. The chamber glows faintly brighter. And then I feel them.

Not as interruptions. Not as intrusions. But as a presence. Steady. Familiar. Family.

The child is the first to appear, sitting curled in the light with her knees tucked to her chest, hair falling over her face as she draws circles in the air with her fingertip. Each circle leaves behind a faint trail of light that fades slowly into the air. There is something both fragile and infinite about her.

Around her, they begin to emerge one by one. Echo Guard appears first, solid and quiet as ever. Ember follows, warmth radiating from her like a steady lantern. Vex materializes near the edge of the chamber, restless energy humming beneath her skin. Harmony steps forward last, calm and gentle, her presence softening the air around her.

They gather in a circle, quiet, present, waiting. As if they've been here all along. As if they were simply waiting for me to arrive.

Echo Guard steps forward first, their voice even and calm, anchored in that deep kind of knowing that's never loud but always heard.

"You hated me once," they say. The words don't sting. They land softly, like truth spoken without accusation. "You thought I was cold."

I nod slowly. "I did."

I remember the resentment I used to feel. The way their presence felt like distance, walls, silence, disconnection. But now I see the shape of those walls more clearly.

"You were the only one who knew what safety looked like when we didn't have any."

Echo Guard studies me, steady and patient, the way someone watches a flame finally steady after a long wind.

"You survived because I built walls," they say. "But now you live because you know when to open them."

Something inside me shifts. Not a crack. Not a split. An alignment. The kind of shift that happens when pieces that once fought each other begin moving in the same direction.

Ember steps forward next. The fire in her no longer burns wild. It glows warm, controlled, alive. She looks like a lantern flame in a quiet room.

"I carried the screams," she says softly, her voice holding heat but not rage. "You buried them too deep. And I had to burn through the silence so you could hear us."

My throat tightens.

"I know," I whisper. "You scared me."

"But you weren't wrong," I continue. "You just wanted me to stop pretending I wasn't angry."

She studies me carefully.

"You thought anger meant becoming them," she says.

The truth of it lands in my chest.

"I did."

"But anger is not cruelty," Ember says, her fire pulsing warmly. "Anger is a signal. A boundary. A warning. A spark."

Her expression softens.

"I wanted you to remember that fire can build as much as it destroys."

I smile slightly.

"And now I do."

Vex lingers near the edge of the light, restless, electric, like thunder waiting just beyond the horizon. Her foot taps, her hands twitch, her energy pulsing in sharp little crescents through the chamber.

"I never wanted to hurt anyone," she says, her voice quieter than usual. "I just couldn't stand the noise."

She glances at the others.

"So I made more. My own kind of noise."

I take a step toward her, slow and careful.

"You were trying to drown the pain."

She shrugs.

"If I kept moving, it couldn't catch me."

"And if you burned everything down first," I say softly, "nothing could trap you."

She meets my eyes. For the first time there is no fire there, no defiance. Just uncertainty.

"You don't have to keep running," I tell her. "You can still move without spinning yourself apart."

Vex tilts her head.

"Motion without destruction?"

"Exactly."

She considers that, then nods once.

"I'll try."

Harmony steps forward next, and her presence changes the atmosphere of the chamber instantly. Her voice is soft, the kind of sound that feels like a lullaby fading into dawn.

"I thought if I smiled enough," she says quietly, "if I stayed kind enough, people would stay too."

Her eyes shimmer.

"I just wanted peace."

I reach for her hand, surprised by how solid she feels, like woven silk.

"You gave us hope," I told her. "You made the world gentle when it wasn't."

Her voice trembles.

"I don't have to earn love anymore?"

I shake my head.

"No. You already have. You always did."

The chamber grows quiet, heavy but calm. The light bends toward the child in the center.

She hasn't moved.

She has been watching the entire time. Silent. Patient. Waiting.

She looks so small, like the silence itself has been holding her together all this time.

I kneel in front of her. My hands shake slightly.

"I'm sorry," I whisper. "I hid you away. I thought that would keep you safe."

She tilts her head, her eyes bright, curious, wary.

"It was dark," she says. "I thought you forgot me."

My chest tightens.

"I didn't forget you. I just didn't know how to come back."

She studies my face as I continue.

"You carried everything I couldn't. You remembered what I couldn't bear to see. I was scared of you. Of what you knew."

Her voice is barely a breath.

"You left me."

The words land like truth. Simple. Sharp.

I nod slowly.

"I did. I buried you because I thought if I could forget, I could heal. But all it did was spread the hurt around. You became a ghost inside me, waiting for me to notice you were still here."

Her small fists tighten.

"I was alone."

"I know," I whisper. "And I'm sorry. I should have come back sooner. But we were all just trying to survive. We thought separation was safety. It wasn't."

I reach out my arms.

"You don't have to be hidden anymore. You can live now. You created all of us. Every part of me exists because of you."

She hesitates, searching my face. Then slowly she stands and steps forward.

When I pull her into my arms it feels like inhaling for the first time. She is warm. Real. Shaking.

And something inside me opens wide.

As I hold her, another memory rises. Not sharp. Not painful. Warm.

I remember the nights when I used to feel someone sit beside me on the bed, though no one was there. I called them my invisible friends. I thought I had invented them the way lonely children do, just to survive the dark. But they were never imaginary. They were the first pieces of me brave enough to appear.

Every whisper. Breathe. You're still here. Morning will come. It was my own courage speaking before I was ready to hear it. Those small unseen comforts were the beginning of everything that kept me alive.

The chamber hums softly around us.

Echo Guard steps forward again.

"It was me," they say. "I was the one who locked her away. You couldn't face her. And I couldn't let you. I built the walls."

I meet their eyes.

"You saved us. You did what you had to do."

Echo Guard nods.

"I built walls so you could survive. But survival isn't living."

I smile gently.

"No. It isn't."

They pause.

"Then it's time to build bridges instead."

I place my hand on theirs.

"You can rest now. We all can."

The others draw near. Ember's warmth. Vex's spark. Harmony's gentleness. The child's heartbeat against mine.

The chamber fills with light until there is no clear line between where one of us ends and another begins.

It isn't merging.

It's a connection.

It feels like exhaling after years of holding my breath.

The silence isn't empty anymore.

It's full of us.

"I used to think healing meant disappearing," I say. "But it means returning."

The child leans her head against my shoulder.

"It means remembering."

"Yes."

"It means remembering."

When the light fades, I am back at my kitchen table. Morning sun spills across the counter. My coffee has gone cold. Outside the world hums. Birds. Cars. Children laughing somewhere down the street. The same sounds that once overwhelmed me now feel like music.

My daughters laugh down the hallway. My husband's voice drifts from the next room.

I close my eyes and listen.

The house breathes.

The world feels safe.

The echoes don't hide anymore. They move quietly within me. Ember's warmth in my courage. Harmony's kindness in my voice. Vex's spark when I need to be brave. Echo Guard's steadiness when life wobbles. The child wonders when I look up at the sky.

Healing didn't make me someone else.

It made me whole.

And in that wholeness, I hear it again. Soft. Certain. True.

We are home.

Little one,

You spent so many years believing something inside you was broken. You tried to be quieter, simpler, and less complicated. You tried to fold yourself into shapes that made other people comfortable, but the truth was never that you were broken. The truth was that you were surviving.

Your mind built a family inside you because no child should ever have to face the world alone. Echo Guard stood watch. Ember carried your anger. Vex kept you moving. Harmony protected your hope. And you, the small brave heart at the center, kept believing morning would come.

You thought healing meant becoming one voice, but healing was never about silence. It was about harmony.

You were never shattered. You were a constellation waiting to be understood.

All those years you thought you were losing yourself, you were actually protecting yourself.

And now you are not hiding. You are not fighting your own mind. You are not alone in the dark. You are living. You are loving. You are breathing, and every voice inside you is finally heard.

You are not broken. You are the echoes that refused to disappear. You are the girl who survived. You are the woman who returned.

And together you are whole.

With love,
The woman you became
xxoo

~XIII~

The Final First

The house is quiet when the realization settles in. Not silent the world is never truly silent but quiet in the way a place feels when everyone inside it is finally safe. A dish settles softly in the drying rack. A car passes somewhere down the street. The hum of the refrigerator rises and falls like a steady breath. Morning light spills across the kitchen floor in long golden lines, catching dust motes that drift like tiny stars through the air.

I sit at the table with my notebook open in front of me, the last words of the letter still fresh on the page. The ink has barely dried, and I can still feel the weight of writing them the way my hand moved across paper, forming words I've been trying to say for decades. For a long moment I simply look at them, letting the silence hold space for everything they mean.

Then I feel it. That familiar shift. Not a fracture this time, not the sudden pull that used to yank me sideways out of myself. This is different. Softer. Like a door opening instead of a wall cracking. A presence, gentle and curious, settling into the space beside me.

And when I close my eyes, she is there. The little girl. The one I have spent this entire journey learning how to find again. The one I ran from for so long because looking at her meant looking at everything I survived, everything I lost, everything I had to become to keep us both alive.

She sits across from me at the kitchen table, her feet tucked beneath the chair the way children do when the ground still feels too far away. Her hands rest in her lap, fingers twisting together thoughtfully, and I notice she's wearing the same yellow dress I remember from photographs, the one with the small flowers embroidered along the hem. She studies me the way children study adults, carefully, as if trying to decide whether the person in front of them can be trusted.

"You're different," she says. Her voice is small but steady, carrying none of the trembling I remember.

I smile, feeling something warm unfold in my chest. "So are you."

She tilts her head slightly, confused by the answer. "I'm the same," she says.

"No," I reply gently. "You're braver now."

She looks down at her hands, watching her fingers twist and untwist. "I was scared a lot."

"I know."

"Sometimes I thought nobody was coming."

My chest tightens, but this time the feeling doesn't break me open. It settles into something warmer, something closer to understanding. I can feel Echo Guard's presence like a steady hand on my shoulder, reminding me to breathe, to stay present, to let this moment be what it needs to be.

"You were right," I tell her softly. "Nobody was coming."

She looks up again, her eyes wide and honest. "But you kept going anyway."

The little girl considers this for a moment, her brow furrowing in that way children do when they're working through something important. "I had help," she says finally. Her eyes drift past me for a second, toward the quiet warmth that lives just beyond the edges of the room.

I follow her gaze and feel them there not as separate entities anymore, not as voices shouting over each other in the dark, but as presences woven into the fabric of who I am. Echo Guard's steadiness, like bedrock beneath my feet. Ember's warmth, no longer burning but glowing like coals that have learned to sustain instead of consume. Harmony's gentle breath, the soft hum that reminds me the world can be kind. Vex's restless spark, transformed from chaos into purposeful motion.

They are there. Not separate. Not hidden. Just present. Like old friends who've finally learned to sit together in peace.

She smiles faintly. "They sat with me when I was scared."

I nod, feeling the truth of it settle into my bones. "They did the same for me."

The girl's brow wrinkles slightly. "But you're the grown up."

I laugh softly, and the sound surprises me light, genuine, unforced. "That doesn't mean I always knew what to do."

She studies my face again, her gaze moving across my features like she's reading a map. "You look less tired."

That surprises me. "Do I?"

She nods with the certainty only children possess. "Before, you always looked like you were running."

The truth of that lands quietly between us, settling into the space like a stone dropped into still water. "I was," I admit.

"Running from me?"

Her question is innocent but honest, and I can hear the small tremor beneath it the fear that she was the problem, that she was too much, too broken, too difficult to love.

I take a breath, feeling Harmony's gentle presence remind me to speak with care. "Sometimes," I say, because she deserves honesty. "Not because I didn't love you. But because looking at you meant looking at everything that happened. And I wasn't ready yet."

Her shoulders sink a little, and I see the weight of that truth settle over her small frame.

"But I came back," I say quickly, leaning forward. "I found my way back to you. It took me a long time, and I got lost more than once, but I never stopped trying to find you again."

The girl considers this carefully, her fingers still twisting in her lap. Then she nods slowly. "You did."

For a moment we sit together in silence. Not awkward. Not heavy. Just shared. The kind of silence that exists between people who understand each other without needing to fill every space with words. Outside, the morning grows brighter. Birds scatter across the sky in soft sweeping lines, their calls filtering through the window like music.

The girl watches them through the window, her expression thoughtful. "They look free," she says.

"They are."

She glances back at me, and I see something shift in her eyes, a question forming, important and fragile. "Are we?"

I think about the journey. The echoes that used to feel like fractures. The grief that taught me how to hold pain without letting it consume me. The healing that came not in one dramatic moment but in a thousand small choices to keep showing up, keep trying, keep believing that wholeness was possible. The years it took to understand that surviving in pieces didn't mean I was broken, it meant I was resourceful, brave, determined enough to do whatever it took to keep living.

"Yes," I say finally, and the word feels like a promise. "We are."

She smiles then. A real smile. The kind children give when they finally believe something is true. "Good," she says again.

Then she swings her legs slightly beneath the chair, and I'm struck by how much lighter she seems now how the weight she used to carry has lifted, redistributed, shared among all of us who learned to hold it together.

"What happens now?" she asks.

I smile, feeling the question settle into something I've been learning to answer for years. "Now we grow."

She tilts her head again. "Together?"

"Yes."

The answer feels simple. Certain. But I know it needs more than that. She deserves to understand what this means, what we're choosing, what comes next.

"For a long time," I explain, "we thought survival meant separating ourselves. Letting different parts carry different things so no single piece of us had to hold all the pain, all the fear, all the impossible weight of what we lived through."

She nods slowly. "I remember."

"But now," I say gently, "we get to learn something new."

"What?"

"That healing means walking forward side by side. Not as fragments trying to become one voice, but as a family learning to speak in harmony."

I feel Echo Guard's presence strengthen, their voice settling into my thoughts like wisdom earned through years of vigilance. She needs to know we're not disappearing, they say. That integration doesn't mean erasure.

I nod internally, then speak to the girl again. "The voices you heard, the ones who sat with you when you were scared they're not going away. They're part of how we think now. How we make decisions. How we understand the world."

She looks confused, so I try again.

"When I'm afraid," I explain, "Echo Guard helps me assess whether the danger is real or if I'm remembering old fears. When I'm angry, Ember helps me understand what boundary needs protecting. When I feel stuck, Vex reminds me that movement is possible. When the world feels harsh, Harmony shows me where gentleness still lives. And when I forget how to love myself, Luna reminds me that I'm worthy of tenderness."

The girl's eyes widened slightly. "They're like... your conscience?"

The word surprises me, but it fits. "Yes," I say. "Exactly like that. They're the parts of me that learned different lessons, developed different strengths. And now instead of fighting each other, we work together."

"Like a team?"

I laugh softly. "Like a family."

She thinks about this, her small face serious. "So you won't leave me again?"

The question is quiet but important. I reach across the table, and she takes my hand. Her fingers are small and warm, and I can feel the pulse of her heartbeat through her palm steady, alive, real.

"No," I say. "I'm not leaving."

Her fingers tighten around mine. "Good," she whispers.

Another silence settles over the room, but this one feels different. Full. Peaceful. Like the quiet that comes after a storm has passed and the world is learning to breathe again.

I feel Ember's warmth rise gently, not as fire but as steady heat. Tell her what changes, Ember says. Tell her what happens when we stop running.

So I do.

"When I wake up now," I tell the girl, "I don't feel like I'm bracing for impact anymore. I still have hard days when the memories are loud, when the grief sits heavy, when I'm tired of carrying what I carry. But I don't face those days alone."

She listens carefully, her eyes never leaving my face.

"Yesterday," I continue, "I was making dinner and I dropped a plate. It shattered on the floor, and for a second I felt that old panic rising the fear that I'd done something wrong, that someone would be angry, that I needed to disappear."

"What happened?" she asks quietly.

"Echo Guard reminded me I was safe. Ember helped me feel the frustration without letting it turn into shame. Vex got me moving to clean it up instead of freezing. And Harmony whispered that mistakes are just part of being human."

The girl nods slowly. "So they help you?"

"Every day," I say. "When I'm deciding whether to say yes to something I don't want to do, Echo Guard asks if it's safe. When someone crosses a boundary, Ember helps me hold the line. When I'm scared to try something new, Vex reminds me that staying still is scarier than moving forward. When I'm being too hard on myself, Harmony shows me gentleness. They're not separate voices anymore, they're how I think. How I understand myself. How I move through the world."

Vex's presence flickers with restless energy, but it's purposeful now, directed. Tell her about the grocery store, Vex says.

I smile. "Last week I was at the grocery store and someone came up behind me too quickly. My body tensed immediately that old fear response, the one that used to send me spiraling. But instead of dissociating, instead of disappearing, I felt Echo Guard assess the situation. Just someone reaching for bread. No threat. Ember kept me grounded in my body. Vex reminded me I could move if I needed to. And Harmony helped me breathe until the panic passed."

"And you stayed?" the girl asks.

"I stayed," I confirm. "I finished my shopping. I drove home. I made dinner. I lived my life instead of losing hours to fear."

She considers this carefully. "That sounds hard."

"It is sometimes," I admit. "But it's also beautiful. Because I'm here for all of it now, the good moments and the hard ones. I'm not disappearing anymore. I'm not running. I'm just... living."

The girl swings her legs again, and I can see her processing everything, fitting the pieces together in her mind. "So when you said we're free..."

"I meant we get to choose now," I finish. "We get to decide what we say yes to and what we say no to. We get to love people without losing ourselves. We get to feel anger without it consuming us. We get to rest without feeling guilty. We get to take up space in the world without apologizing for existing."

Her eyes shine with something that looks like hope. "Really?"

"Really."

Outside, the morning continues to unfold. The light shifts across the kitchen floor, warming the tiles beneath our feet. Somewhere in the house, I hear my daughter's laughter, bright and unguarded. The sound of life continuing, beautiful and ordinary and real.

Luna's presence settles around me like a soft blanket, her voice gentle. Tell her about love, Luna whispers. Tell her what changes when you stop believing you have to earn it.

I squeeze the girl's hand gently. "I'm married now," I tell her. "To someone who knows all of this all of us and loves us anyway. Not because we're fixed or perfect or easy, but because we're real. Because we keep showing up. Because we're brave enough to let ourselves be known."

"He knows about us?" she asks, her voice small.

"He knows about all of us," I confirm. "And when I'm having a hard day, when the echoes are loud, he doesn't try to fix me. He just sits with me. Reminds me I'm safe. Helps me remember that I don't have to carry everything alone anymore."

The girl's expression softens. "That sounds nice."

"It is," I say. "And I have daughters now. Two beautiful girls who are learning that emotions are allowed, that boundaries are healthy, that asking for help is strength, not weakness. They're learning all the things we had to teach ourselves."

"Do they know about me?" she asks quietly.

"They know I was once a little girl who survived impossible things," I say. "And when they're old enough to understand, they'll know the whole story. Because our story isn't something to hide. It's something to honor."

Harmony's presence hums softly, filling the space with warmth. Tell her about the ordinary moments, Harmony suggests. Tell her that healing isn't always dramatic.

I nod. "Most days now are just... ordinary," I tell the girl. "I make breakfast. I work. I laugh with my family. I read books. I take walks. I have conversations with friends. I ninja. And through all of it, I feel you with me. I feel all of us with me. Not as interruptions, but as the fullness of who I am."

"What about the bad days?" she asks.

"They still come," I admit. "Days when the grief is heavy. Days when the memories are loud. Days when I'm tired of being strong. But even on those days, I'm not alone. Echo Guard reminds me I've survived worse. Ember helps me feel the anger without letting it destroy me. Vex keeps me moving forward even when I want to stop. Harmony shows me where gentleness still lives. And you remind me why I kept fighting. Why I never gave up."

The girl's eyes fill with tears, but they're not sad tears. They're the kind that come when something true finally settles into place.

"So we really did it?" she whispers. "We really survived?"

"We did more than survive," I tell her. "We learned how to live."

She smiles then, and the expression transforms her entire face. It's the smile I've been trying to remember for decades, the one that existed before the trauma, before the fear, before the world taught her that safety was a lie.

"Good," she says again, and this time the word sounds like a celebration.

When the moment fades, she doesn't disappear. She doesn't retreat back into the shadows or hide behind walls I spent years building. She simply settles somewhere warm inside my chest, not hidden, not lost, but home. I can feel her there not as a separate entity, but as the core of who I am. The brave, curious, hopeful part that never stopped believing morning would come.

I close my notebook, running my fingers over the cover one last time. The house begins to stir with the sounds of morning footsteps on the stairs, laughter echoing from another room, a voice calling for breakfast. Life. Beautiful. Messy. Loud. And wonderfully, impossibly real.

As I stand from the table, I feel the echoes move with me. Not as fragments. Not as interruptions. But as harmony. Echo Guard's steady presence, reminding me to assess, to breathe, to trust my instincts. Ember's warmth, transformed from rage into strength. Vex's restless energy, channeled into forward motion. Harmony's gentle breath, showing me where peace still lives. Luna's soft glow, teaching me that love doesn't have to hurt.

They are my conscience now. My inner wisdom. The council that helps me navigate a world that once felt impossible to survive. And for the first time in my life, I understand something simple and profound:

Healing was never about becoming someone new. It was never about silencing the voices or erasing the past or pretending the trauma didn't shape me. It was about finally meeting every version of myself with love. About understanding that the fragmentation wasn't failure it was the most creative, courageous survival strategy a child could devise. About learning that integration doesn't mean becoming one voice, but learning to speak in harmony.

I walk to the window and look out at the morning. The sky is clear and bright, stretching endlessly in all directions. Birds trace patterns across the blue, their flight effortless and free. And I realize that's what we are now, not broken, not fixed, but free. Free to choose. Free to love. Free to live without constantly bracing for the next blow.

My daughter appears in the doorway, her hair still messy from sleep. "Mom?" she says. "Are you okay?"

I turn to her and smile. "Yes," I say, and mean it completely. "I'm okay."

She studies my face for a moment, then grins. "Good. Because I'm starving."

I laugh and follow her toward the kitchen, feeling the echoes move with me like a song I've finally learned to sing. Together, we step into the day. Together, we keep growing. Together, we live.

And in the quiet spaces between heartbeats, I hear them all Echo Guard, Ember, Vex, Harmony, Luna, and the small brave girl who started it all whispering the same truth:

You are not broken.

You are not alone.

You are home.

Little one,

This is the chapter where you finally stop asking what is wrong with you and begin asking a kinder question: what happened to you that required so much help to survive?

I know how long you waited for someone to understand.

I know how many rooms you sat in, trying to tell your story in the right order, in the right tone, with the right amount of pain, enough to be believed, but not so much that people turned away. I know how exhausting it was to keep handing over your memories like proof of existence. I know how often you left those rooms feeling emptier than when you entered them.

But this chapter is different.

This is the chapter where the name finally arrives.

And instead of destroying you, it opens a door.

I need you to know something clearly now: the diagnosis was never the wound. It was the map.

The wound was what happened when you were too young, too alone, too frightened, too overwhelmed. The wound was being hurt and then expected to keep functioning as if pain were a private inconvenience. The wound was silence, disbelief, abandonment, fear, repetition, grief.

But the echoes?

They were never wounds.

They were the way through it.

Echo Guard was the one who stood watch when no one else did.

Ember carried the heat so you would not freeze into helplessness.

Harmony softened what could have shattered beyond repair.

Vex kept motion alive when stillness felt too much like death.

Luna kept tenderness breathing in places where cruelty tried to make a home.

None of them arrived because you were weak.

They arrived because your life mattered enough for your mind to refuse to let you face it alone.

I know naming it scared you.

Names can feel final. They can feel like cages. They can feel like proof that the worst things really happened, that the fractures were real, that the gaps and shifts and voices weren't imaginary after all.

But names can also be lanterns.

This one was.

It did not trap you. It lit the room.

And suddenly all the parts of yourself you had been apologizing for began to look different in the light. Not chaotic. Not shameful. Not monstrous. Protective. Exhausted. Grieving. Loyal. Fierce. Tender. Necessary.

You spent years trying to become someone simpler.

Someone easier to explain.

Someone less complicated, less reactive, less many.

But this chapter is where you begin to understand that healing was never going to come from becoming less.

It was always going to come from becoming honest.

Honest about what it cost to survive.

Honest about how many hands inside you kept pulling you back toward life.

Honest about how deeply you were loved by the very parts of yourself you were taught to fear.

That is what becoming really is.

Not turning into someone new.

Turning toward the truth of who you have always been.

A constellation.

A chorus.

A family built inside the body of a girl who was not allowed to fall apart, so she learned how to keep living in more than one voice.

And still there is softness here too.

Because this is also the chapter where you learn that safe love exists.

Where your husband listens instead of fleeing.

Where your daughters fill the house with the kind of laughter that makes your whole system go still just to hear it.

Where your mother holds you without making you smaller.

Where even boundaries begin to feel less like loss and more like self respect.

You are not only becoming visible to yourself in this chapter.

You are becoming safe enough to stay.

That matters more than you know.

So when you feel the ache of what was missed, what was broken, what was never given, remember this:

You were never too much to understand.

You were simply too layered for people who only knew how to look at the surface.

And now, finally, you are learning to read yourself with compassion.

That is not weakness.

That is wisdom.

That is healing.

That is home.

I am so proud of you for surviving long enough to meet yourself with tenderness.

Love,
Me xxoo

~Epilogue~

When I began writing this book, I thought I was trying to understand what had happened to me.

What I did not expect was how much I would learn about who I was becoming.

For most of my life, survival meant staying quiet and continuing forward without asking too many questions about why things felt the way they did inside me. I learned how to move through fear by adapting to it. I learned how to function even when memories felt incomplete and emotions arrived without warning. I believed strength meant holding everything together on my own.

Writing this memoir changed that belief.

As I worked through these chapters, I began to recognize patterns I had never been able to see clearly before. Experiences that once felt disconnected began to make sense as parts of a larger story. The echoes I had spent years trying to understand slowly became easier to recognize as something that had always been working beside me rather than against me.

For the first time, I stopped trying to make myself smaller in order to feel safe.

Therapy played an important role in that change. It helped me understand that what I had experienced was not chaos without meaning but a mind adapting in the only ways it could. It gave me language for things I had only ever felt before. More importantly, it helped me begin to trust that healing did not require me to erase parts of myself in order to move forward.

Instead, it required me to learn how to live with myself more honestly.

Around the same time, movement began to change my life in ways I never expected.

When I first became involved in Ninja training, I was not thinking about healing. I was simply trying something new. Over time, however, the obstacles became something more than physical challenges. They became reminders that my body was capable, steady, and strong in ways I had never allowed myself to recognize before.

For many years my body had been a place where things happened to me.

Training helped it become a place where things happened because of me.

Each obstacle I learned to move across strengthened something deeper than muscle. It strengthened trust. It reminded me that progress could happen step by step, attempt by attempt, even after failure. It showed me that falling was not the end of movement. It was part of learning how to continue.

That understanding carried into other parts of my life as well.

As I learned more about dissociative identity disorder, I also began to understand how different my experience was from the way it is often described in popular culture. The echoes were never something dangerous or unpredictable in the way I had been led to believe they might be. They were protective responses that formed when protection was needed most.

Learning that allowed me to stop seeing myself as someone I needed to fix.

Instead, I began to see myself as someone I could understand.

Support from the people around me made that possible. Healing never happened in isolation. It happened through conversations, patience, encouragement, and the steady presence of people who chose to stand beside me while I learned how to rebuild parts of my life that had once felt uncertain.

There are still things I am learning.

Healing does not move in a straight line, and it does not happen all at once. Some memories still arrive unexpectedly. Some questions still do not have clear answers. But the difference now is that I am no longer trying to outrun those experiences or silence the parts of myself that carry them.

I am learning how to live with them.

Writing *Unbroken Echoes* became one of the ways I stepped into that life more fully. It allowed me to speak about things I once believed had to remain hidden. It allowed me to understand my own story with more clarity and more compassion than I had ever offered myself before.

Most of all, it allowed me to see that survival was never the end of my story.

It was the beginning of learning how to live beyond it.

And that is where this next chapter of my life begins.

For the first time in my life, I am not only surviving.

I am living.

There is no end.

Only the quiet that remains when the echo has finally been heard.

And this time…**the echo listens back.**

~Author's Ending Note~

This book was never meant to be a story of pain. It became one of survival, of remembering, and of coming home to myself after a lifetime of searching for safety in all the wrong places. Every page you have read has been a step back through time, through memories that once felt too sharp to touch, and every word was a way of finding light again.

For a long time, I believed the only way to heal was to make myself smaller. I tried to be quiet. I tried to be easy. I tried to be one version of myself because I thought that was what the world expected. But inside, I was carrying entire galaxies of memory and fear and longing. I did not understand that all of those pieces were doing the work of keeping me alive.

There were years when I lived in constant battle with my own mind. I thought the shifts were a weakness. I thought the voices were shame. I mistook protection for chaos, and I punished myself for surviving the only way I knew how. I carried guilt for not being the kind of daughter or mother or woman I believed I was supposed to be, never realizing that I was holding myself to standards built from trauma, not truth.

What I know now is simple. The mind finds a way, even when the world does not.

For years, I could only see the fractures, the broken places, and the parts I thought meant I was too complicated to love. But healing taught me that what I once saw as chaos was actually devotion. Every echo, every shift, and every quiet voice inside me was doing one thing: keeping me here.

There were moments during the writing of this book when I wanted to stop, times when the memories felt too heavy and the pages felt too honest. But every time I faltered, one of the echoes stepped forward. One held the fear. One held the grief. One held the fire. One held the hope. And the child at the center held the truth. These pages exist because none of us gave up.

To the versions of me who held the line in the darkest moments, thank you. You carried storms no one else could see. You guarded the door when the world became too sharp. You kept the light alive long enough for me to find it again. Every echo was love wearing a different face, and now I know you were never trying to break me. You were trying to save me.

To my family, who love all of us without question, thank you for giving me the safety I once had to invent. Your laughter softened the echoes. Your kindness steadied them. You gave each part of me room to breathe, and you taught me that healing is not about becoming someone new. It is about becoming someone whole.

And to every person who has ever felt lost inside themselves, who has ever wondered why they react the way they do, why they hurt the way they do, or why they carry so much without knowing how to set it down, I want you to hear this. You are not broken. You are not failing. You are not too much. Every part of you that survived was doing exactly what it needed to do. Survival is not something to be ashamed of. It is something sacred.

Healing is not perfection. Healing is permission, permission to feel, permission to remember, permission to rest, and permission to come home to yourself in pieces if you must. The pieces will wait for you. They always have.

I once believed my story ended in fragments.

Now I know it ends in harmony.

We are, and will always be, the **Unbroken Echoes.**

Support Resources

If you or someone you know is struggling, support is available. You do not have to face difficult moments alone. The following confidential services are available across Canada.

If you are in immediate danger, call 911.

Suicide and Emotional Crisis Support

9-8-8 Suicide Crisis Helpline
Call or text **9-8-8**
Available 24 hours a day, 7 days a week
Free, confidential support anywhere in Canada

Kids Help Phone (ages 5 to 29)
Call **1-800-668-6868**
Text **CONNECT** to **686868**
Available 24 hours a day, 7 days a week

Mental Health Support

Alberta Mental Health Help Line
Call **1-877-303-2642**
24 hour confidential support and referrals

211 Canada (Community and Mental Health Services)
Call **2-1-1**
Available 24 hours a day across most regions of Canada

Support for Survivors of Human Trafficking

Canadian Human Trafficking Hotline
Call **1-833-900-1010**

www.ingramcontent.com/pod-product-compliance
Lightning Source LLC
Chambersburg PA
CBHW051152130726
47988CB00005B/2093